PEN AMERICA

Published by PEN America,
an affiliate of PEN International,
the worldwide association of writers
working to advance literature
and defend free expression.

https://pen.org/literature/pen-america-a-journal-for-writers-and-readers/

PEN America: A Journal for Writers and Readers
Issue 20: We the People

PEN America
588 Broadway, Suite 303
New York, NY 10012

This issue is made possible by the generous funding of The Lillian Goldman Charitable Trust.

Printed in the United States of America by McNaughton and Gunn.

Postmaster: Send address changes to
PEN America, c/o PEN America,
588 Broadway, Suite 303,
New York, NY 10012.

Email: journal@pen.org
Phone: (646) 779-4816

COVER IMAGES:
Gabriel Orozco
My Hands Are My Heart, 1991
Silver dye bleach print
Each: 9-1/8 × 12-1/2 in. / 23.2 × 31.8 cm
Courtesy of the Artist and Marian Goodman Gallery

ISBN: 1536-0261
ISSN: 0-934638-57-8

PEN AMERICA

20 | WE THE PEOPLE

EDITOR
M Mark

ASSOCIATE EDITOR
Laura Swearingen-Steadwell

COPY EDITOR
Loren Noveck

EDITORIAL INTERNS
Myra Al-Rahim
Alexandra Frankland
Anthony A. Parks
Naheed Phiroze Patel
Daniela Spencer

LAYOUT/ART EDITOR
Simon M. Sullivan

CONTENTS

11   **THE SILVER SCRAPHEAP** | *Fiction by Anita Augustin, translated by Rachel McNicholl*

13   **TOWARD THE GREAT UNITY** | *Poetry by Sarah V. Schweig*

14   **MUSLIM IN AMERICA** | *Conversation with Ayad Akhtar, Rozina Ali, and Haroon Moghul, with Arun Venugopal*

30   **THE GREAT WALL** *and* **THE WALL** | *Nonfiction by Eliot Weinberger*

37   **SAMIYA SCHMIDT** | *Fiction by Antoine Volodine, translated by Jeffrey Zuckerman*

44   **MAUREEN** | *Fiction by Sara Majka*

47   **LUKIN'S BED** | *Fiction by Vivian Abenshushan, translated by Susan Ouriou*

59   **MAROONED** | *Fiction by Jean Rhys*

61   **THE IMAGINING OF IT** | *Fiction by Jamaica Kincaid*

64   **WRITING IN SHIFTING SPACE** | *Conversation with Kwame Anthony Appiah, Marlon James, Jamaica Kincaid, Valeria Luiselli, and Colum McCann, with Eric Banks*

77   **KYLE & JASON** | *Nonfiction by Marlon James*

81   **DAY PASSES** | *Nonfiction by Anne Enright*

84   **WHITE PEOPLE EATING WHITE FOOD** | *Poetry by francine j. harris*

86   **SIREN, AGAIN** | *Poetry by Gala Mukomolova*

88   **LAST NIGHT, I WOKE UP IN THE WRONG BODY AGAIN** | *Poetry by Tommye Blount*

90   **I WANT SO DESPERATELY TO BE FINISHED WITH DESIRE** | *Poetry by sam sax*

94   **PRONUNCIATION: PART ONE** | *Poetry by Aziza Barnes*

95   **TOLSTOY CAN'T SUE** | *Conversation with Walter Mosley and Boris Akunin, with Keith Gessen*

110   **From CHARCOAL JOE** | *Fiction by Walter Mosley*

115   **MY HANDS ARE MY HEART** | *Conversation with Gabriel Orozco and Colm Tóibín*

137   **EAST TEXAS MACHINERY** | *Nonfiction by Gene Walker*

139   **PRISON BRANDING IN THE AGE OF MASS INCARCERATION** *Nonfiction by Helen Hofling and Timothy Small*

143   **NARRATIVE ANIMALS** | *Conversation with Salman Rushdie and Lila Azam Zanganeh*

153   **GARDENER'S MEMORY** | *Poetry by Catherine LaFleur*

154   **A LIVE DOG BEING BETTER THAN A DEAD LION** | *Poetry by Brigit Pegeen Kelly*

155   **From USING LIFE** | *Fiction by Ahmed Naji, translated by Ben Koerber*

158 **LUNG** | *Graphic Narrative by Josh Trujillo*

172 **BECOMING THE CHAPLAIN** | *Fiction by Ben Kingsley*

175 **MR. LEVI** | *Nonfiction by Jeremy Mulligan*

179 **PHOENIX** | *Fiction by MJ McGinn*

180 **THE SHOOTINGS** | *Fiction by Hubert Mingarelli, translated by Sam Taylor*

183 **THE LAST STAND** | *Fiction by L.P. Sutton*

193 **THE SETTING SUN** | *Memoir by Nate McKowen*

197 **PATRICK STEWART** | *Fiction by Fortunato Salazar*

199 **MASTER FILM** | *Poetry by Solmaz Sharif*

201 **A COVERED UP PAST** | *Nonfiction by Tsering Woeser*

203 **ZOFRAN** | *Poetry by Dilruba Ahmed*

204 **THE STICK** | *Poetry by Nicole Callihan*

207 *Contributors*

217 *Acknowledgments*

"The language of the Constitution...is 'we the people'; not we the white people, not even we the citizens, not we the privileged class, not we the high, not we the low, but we the people."

—FREDERICK DOUGLASS

THE SILVER SCRAPHEAP

Anita Augustin

TRANSLATED BY RACHEL MCNICHOLL

They take everything when the time comes. Everything you have left. Your keys, your furniture, your potted palm. The right to wake up when you like, to go to sleep when you like. The right *not* to eat a bland diet, *not* to take vitamin pills, and the right to take as many sleeping pills as you like.

The right to be lonely.

Then, after they've taken everything, they give you a Life Story form. This is their first gift; others will follow—like the list of leisure activities or the form for your feedback on the last memory training session—but the Life Story form is the first.

It is a gift, so don't be ungrateful, take it easy, stop pretending your potted palm was real, that you were lonely by choice, that your old life was just fine before they took it away.

Just stop it.

Marvelous things, these Life Story forms. It's all in there, what you were in another life. A working woman, active, successful. Your hobbies are all there, the ones you used to have. Cycling, glass painting, model railways. They want to know whether you would have considered yourself more happy than unhappy in the past, whether you suffered from any chronic illnesses or from depression. They even ask what your favorite color is and write *Black* in the box and draw an arrow linking it to the box for *Depression,* where there's a big fat X.

When you say that these days yellow is your favorite color, a warm, nourishing egg-yolk yellow, they couldn't give a shit.

You say: I've given up glass painting and now I'd rather take up martial arts.

No response.

You say: I was more unhappy than happy in the past but now I'd rather be happy, if that can be arranged.

No response.

Then they ask if you can still manage the toilet on your own, how hot or cold you like the water for your wash, and whether you have made adequate provision for your funeral.

So much for the future.

Rachel McNicholl was awarded a 2016 PEN/Heim Translation Grant.

TOWARD THE GREAT UNITY

Sarah V. Schweig

And then I went to seek The Great Unity.
Goodbye, I said, *my family*, as I left them.
I worked for a company in a municipal building.
In a hole, with my belongings, I built a home.

I was young, always returning to the municipal building,
where an iron lamp hung, a flickering vestige of history.
And when I moved my belongings in with a man and out of their hole,
Goodbye, my family. I'll be seeing you. I'll be writing you, I'd said.

It wasn't easy. In their search for meaning, they resemble me, my family.
We want to understand the meaning of experience. Back when poetry
poured from my young body, words brought up history, and seemed to
transcend. Poetry stopped. To the idea of The Great Unity I clung.

Each morning, I walked my body beneath the flickering lamp,
meaning nothing. Words brought up history, and I wrote it down.
It left my memory empty, and I forgot what I meant.
I'll be writing you, I wrote, but could not bear the words.

Poetry stopped in my aging body. Now it carries what remains
of my family: The memory of my young brother, in the face of a man
visiting the home I built with another. Sometimes, rarely, he flickers before me,
that boy, my brother, whom I could never fully record in poetry, in history.

I thought I'd find The Great Unity. It seems there is none.
Now, I kneel down before its flickering idea, and my family
kneels down inside me. All of history brought us here.
Goodbye, I said, *my history*. And then my young brother disappeared.

MUSLIM IN AMERICA

Ayad Akhtar, Rozina Ali, and Haroon Moghul,
with Arun Venugopal

ARUN VENUGOPAL: With the optics of Islam in America, are you constantly recalibrating your relationship as a practicing Muslim in this country, your relationship with your faith, as well as with this country you live in?

HAROON MOGHUL: There comes a time when you start to realize how marginal you are, and how conditional your place is in a society; that's what I feel. The language that's being used on the right is fascist. It's worrying as an American, and it's existentially unsettling as a person of color.

VENUGOPAL: Ayad, you once wrote, "I spent three years living in Europe, and it brought home to me not only how American I am, but how much I love America. There are certain aspects of American life spiritually that will always be a part of who I am." Just curious: When did you write this, and how much do you think that feeling still holds?

AYAD AKHTAR: I have family members who live in other parts of the country, and there are times when it's difficult for them to feel safe to leave the house. So it's hard not to have compassion and a great deal of sadness about all of it. From another perspective, this is a fascinating time to be writing. So I plead the self-involvement of the artist when I think about some of these things. I'm reminded of that quote by Asimov about the anti-intellectualism in American life, succinctly put by this phrase: "My ignorance is as good as your knowledge." That, on some level, seems to define American intellectual life, going back to de Tocqueville. I think we're all grappling with disenfranchisement, or lack of empowerment.

Agency seems to be less and less available to individuals, whether we're people of color, whether we're white middle class, what have you. Actually, the reality of what's happening in this country is that we all have a lot more in common than we realize. But when people get scared, it's very easy to think that somebody else is to blame for that. Someone *is* to blame, but it may not actually be Muslims.

VENUGOPAL: I am curious about the relationship between what's happening in Europe and what's happening here right now. Not too long ago, the political right was fairly isolated from the goings-on across the pond, but increasingly, there is something happening in sync. They're almost going in lockstep in Europe and in America.

You've spent time in Europe, correct, Ayad?

AKHTAR: I hated being in Europe. I love Europe, but I hated it. I lived in France for three years, and I'd never experienced the kind of racism, the sort of naked elitist exclusion, that I experienced when I lived in France. What's happening in Europe is still different in some ways, because there are these ethnocentric identities that are so reified. I think in America folks are *trying* to build toward a consolidated ethnic identity, but in France, you're French or you're not. In Germany, up until the late '80s, you couldn't even be a German citizen until you had consanguinity.

ROZINA ALI: What I find frightening about the United States is there's this entire social project of reimagining America to be "great again" that is not a reaction to the realities that Europe sees. Teju Cole says, "Citizenship is an act of the imagination. I was born American, but I also had to learn how to become American." For a long time, that quote has resonated with me. Now I realize it also applies to these Trump supporters, these white people who have to grapple with an America that is different from what they thought it was, an America in which Muslims are a reality, in which the black community is a lot more vocal: It requires an act of imagination from them that I haven't seen yet.

AKHTAR: In Europe it's embedded in the psyche, because of the gates of Vienna. They stopped the Muslims at the gates of Vienna. In Austria, they still talk about it. The croissant is the celebration of stopping the Moors, stopping the Ottomans, at the gates of Vienna. That affirmation of an ethnocentric identity is deeply embedded in the psyche of European cultures. One of the great modernist French myths is Camus's *The Stranger*, which is about killing an Arab. It's the killing of Arabs and the pillaging of the Muslim world that on some level is the national, galvanizing act of the French culture. That's where the French soul resides. "Égalité, fraternité…" Where? Well, they find it by taking it to the Muslims.

I don't think the United States is quite there yet, because I think multiculturalism is still our embedded core idea, as opposed to something that we're trying to figure out how to do.

MOGHUL: The largest mass rapes in Europe in recent times were of Muslims, of Bosnian Muslim women. About sixty thousand were raped in rape camps about twenty years ago, by white European Christians. That doesn't mean it's indicative or representative of white Europeans or Christianity, but what's interesting beyond that is that white Christians called these Bosnians "Turks" and "foreigners," although they're Slavs and indigenous to Europe. They've been Muslim longer than there have been Protestants in existence. Islam is deeply rooted in Europe, and yet that history is erased. The way it's remembered, as you said, is Islam versus the West.

Central Asian Tatar Muslims settled in Poland and Polish Lithuania in the eleventh century. They fought against the Ottomans on the side of the Polish, and they actually broke the Ottoman siege of Vienna. They were so ethnically similar to Ottoman Turks that they wore feathers in their caps to be distinguished from the Ottomans, so their Christian allies wouldn't accidentally shoot them. Those Tatars, their descendants— there are only about four or five thousand left in Poland—were among the first to take up arms when the Nazis invaded Poland. There's a perception of a uniform Polish Catholic identity, but Muslims have been part of Poland for about a thousand years.

VENUGOPAL: Haroon, you had an article in *Time* a few days ago called "Islamophobia Is Ruining America (But Not How You Think)." So how is Islamophobia actually ruining America?

MOGHUL: The Bush administration, in order to make the case to go to war against Iraq, had to say that Saddam was in bed with Al Qaeda. Or that

Iraq, which was a pulverized country that had gone through a decade and a half of war, was an existential threat to the United States. How is that even possible?

AKHTAR: A decade and a half of war that was supported by us and created by us. The chemical weapons Hussein used were chemical weapons the US government gave him.

MOGHUL: When people linked these things and said, "Al Qaeda, Saddam, they're united," they took advantage of ignorance about Islam and the Middle East. A fringe terrorist movement that was dangerous but localized in Afghanistan became an existential threat from one and a half billion people, a clash of civilizations. As a result, we have spent, in the last thirteen years, two trillion dollars on a war that not only was unnecessary, illegal, and unjustifiable, but led to the deaths of thousands of Americans, hundreds of thousands of Iraqis, and created ISIS. When I say Islamophobia is ruining America, I mean the conflation of anything Muslim with terrorism amps up people's existential fear, so we end up spending money on things that actually make us less safe. I mean, two trillion dollars up until now? Seventy billion dollars a year would pay for everyone in America to go to college for free.

The decision to go to war in Iraq was the greatest foreign policy disaster in American history, because we literally see no way out of it. And ISIS is so dangerous that you can't pretend it doesn't exist. Although, as Ayad was saying, if we use vastly superior weaponry to invade a country five or six times, why are we surprised that apocalyptic death cults result?

When we talk about Islamophobia, and I say, "Well, as a Muslim, I'm discriminated against," the majority of people are like, "Oh, that sucks, but that's not my life." But this *is* your life. Our future has been radically reoriented by Islamophobia.

VENUGOPAL: I'm curious about pop culture. Rozina, you have looked at the imagery we're saturated with. You say a show like *Homeland*, which you've really studied closely, in some ways helped foment the War on Terror.

ALI: *Homeland* tries to fill the narrative gap for Americans and define who Muslims are, what the enemy is, what the other is. It seems nuanced—we think it's nuanced, it has these grey zones. In the Pakistan season, I was really surprised by the episode where Carrie Mathison felt bad about a drone strike that killed about forty people. I thought, Wow, here's this US character feeling bad about the deaths of Muslims, but ultimately, you get to the same point at the end of every season, which is: "This is a dirty war, but this is a good war. We have to fight Muslims."

You can see the repercussions of this. During an intense bombardment of Gaza, people on Fox and CNN and news media across the United States were saying, "Well, the people being bombed are terrorists." How can you have so many terrorists in such a densely populated city as Gaza? In such a place, how can you say no civilians are dying? You're conflating civilians and terrorists and saying, "This is war. And this is the good war." I think this is the message that *Homeland* drills into people over and over again, to the point where the public becomes complicit.

VENUGOPAL: And its number one fan is President Obama, from what I remember.

ALI: Absolutely.

AKHTAR: And if there is any recognition of the error of conflation in the show, it's only to give the lead character a moment of compassion. It's a hermetically sealed system. I mean, it's narrative. You have to have a bad guy. That's telling a story.

VENUGOPAL: Ayad, you told *Esquire* in an interview recently, "I'm not gonna sit here and tell you Muslims are the problem. But I'm also not gonna sit here and tell you they're not the problem. We're all in this together and we're all the problem. It's not just them and it's not just us. But nobody wants to hear that."

AKHTAR: Yeah, I still don't think they want to hear that.

VENUGOPAL: What are you hearing? You have maybe a complex relationship with the community—is that a good phrase to use?

AKHTAR: Yeah, perhaps.

VENUGOPAL: In your play *Disgraced*, you had a Muslim character closeted in his faith?

AKHTAR: Not really closeted, more lapsed, renounced. Somebody at profound odds with the fact that he comes from a Muslim background, preemptively dealing with the Islamophobic environment by saying, "Screw that stuff. I hate that stuff. I'm going to tell you everything that's wrong with it so that you understand that's not who I am." But in this environment, even that act of proclaiming one's citizenship with the non-Muslim world is not enough, because once a Muslim, always a Muslim. That's basically the story of *Disgraced*.

VENUGOPAL: This play does phenomenally well. How many productions are going on or have been?

AKHTAR: It's probably more than twenty in this country this year, and more than that next year in this country. And around the world, I mean, everywhere. It's being done everywhere.

I think it can be an exciting experience for the audience. People think they're walking in to watch a show which is going to make them feel like Muslims are humans or something. I didn't write it to show that Muslims are humans; I don't take my job as an artist as PR. But I think the play oddly leaves people the freedom to feel whatever they want. So if they walk in hating Islam, they can leave hating Islam. I think they find that very surprising.

I wrote *Disgraced* five years ago. There's a kind of degradation of public discourse in the play, the way people are speaking to each other, which even five years ago, I would never have imagined could exist anywhere except on the stage. But now people go to see the play, and they're watching on stage what they're seeing back home on television, or they're hearing in coffee shops. I think the play was prescient about something in American life that ultimately had nothing to do with Islam.

At the end of the day, I don't think you can have a show that's being done that often if it's just of anthropological interest. Audiences have got to feel like they're getting something that touches them where they live and breathe. Am I answering your question?

VENUGOPAL: Yeah, but I'm curious. You're saying that you didn't have the agenda that one may ascribe to an artist, but we've seen what an image or a show can do negatively to perpetuate certain ideas about a group of people.

AKHTAR: But *Homeland*'s trying to get you to give them something. It's not art. It's operating within a system where it is trying to get you to stay in the show and then give the producers a rating which leads to advertising. When I wrote *Disgraced*, I didn't have an objective like that. My objective was not to get something from the audience by giving them something that they want or don't want. As an artist, I don't have a transactional relationship with them. I'm not saying art's better, I'm just saying it's different. Within a market economy, there's a denatured vocation for art where we're constantly looking for its social utility. Advocacy and PR are what art ends up being for a lot of people. For me, that's not what it is.

VENUGOPAL: But if someone who's never met a Muslim—which most Americans have not, we're told—goes in and spends an hour and a half with even this highly flawed Muslim person, what can one hope—

AKHTAR: See, this is my problem. If you're a writer of color, and you write an antihero, you're writing a stereotype. If you're a white writer writing a white antihero, it's Don Draper or Tony Soprano. Your question—with all due respect—it's really not a question. You're talking about optics. That's not the mandate or purview or destiny of art! That has nothing to do with why we do it and why audiences go to something. To be renewed and connected to the source of a kind of vitality and aliveness, to experience, to emotion, to sensation—that's what it's about!

VENUGOPAL: Even if you say, "I'm not an agenda-setting kind of a writer, I'm an artist," surely there are experiences which people have that are different from that.

AKHTAR: Art is ultimately a humble thing. You write something, and then people see it, and then they think about it for a day, if you did a really good job, and if you didn't, they stop thinking about it after five minutes.
W. E. B. Du Bois, the great cultural theorist of the black American

experience, talked about double consciousness, where you have minority cultures who see their experience through the eyes of a majority culture. And Langston Hughes and Zora Neale Hurston had the debate during the Harlem Renaissance about the responsibility of representing your people versus the responsibility to the artistic. This is a long-standing debate within minority communities. From my perspective, I don't write from a place of double consciousness. A lot of Muslims come to see my work, and some of them read *American Dervish* and they put it down after page two because the character eats pork, and why would you ever read a book about a Muslim guy that eats pork? But I'm not writing from the place where I'm worried about what white people are going to think of Muslims. That's not my job.

VENUGOPAL: Haroon, what's the name of your project? It's a storytelling initiative, am I right? What is it called again?

MOGHUL: Avenue Meem.

VENUGOPAL: What is Avenue Meem, and what do you do?

MOGHUL: It's just a way to make money. I mean—to show diversity in the Muslim community.

AKHTAR: How's that working out for you?

MOGHUL: Not well. I think I believe in art now.

In the Muslim world, they have these things called mosalsalat, these serials they do during Ramadan where there's a different episode every night. A friend of mine and I decided to do our own version for Ramadan, a minute a night for thirty nights, and I told the story of how I almost became Catholic. I thought it was a chance to talk about something that was meaningful to me, that was part of my own spiritual journey. I wasn't looking for any kind of epiphany or conversion narrative, or this simplistic kind of thing. Just part of my life experience. I grew up in a town where there was one Jewish student, and then there was me, so you knew who was hanging out with who on Christmas. It was me, him, and that Chinese restaurant. It was like a Ralph Peters novel.

In the story, I try to describe what I went through, and what I think a lot of immigrant-origin Muslims go through, that you grow up in places where you're very isolated and very alone. I found in the Catholics around me something I couldn't find in the Muslim community around me.

ALI: Which is what?

MOGHUL: Intimacy, I think. Warmth. A feeling of being rooted in something that actually responded to my identity. A lot of Muslims will say that they find the Trinity irrational, that's a very common argument, but I didn't buy that. If God wants to send a book to someone, why can't he send a part of himself as someone? It's God. By definition, it's not supposed to make sense.

VENUGOPAL: He's got a lot of choices, yes.

MOGHUL: Right?

VENUGOPAL: A very humble objective: You just want to tell stories.

MOGHUL: Yeah.

VENUGOPAL: Are Muslim leaders, theologians, trying to address the political realities in a more elevated way than they might have five or ten years ago?

MOGHUL: There's an unnerving strain of apocalyptic sentiment. ISIS's magazine is called *Dabiq*, a place in Muslim eschatology (which is as contentious as Christian eschatology) where allegedly there will be a great battle between the Muslims and Crusaders or Franks. Al Qaeda in Syria's media outlet is called The White Minaret, which is where it's believed Jesus will descend at the end of time. These movements are deeply inflected by an idea that they are on the side of Jesus, which is really weird.

VENUGOPAL: Did you want to add something to that, Ayad?

AKHTAR: There are complexities to be discussed. I did an event with the

Council on Foreign Relations, and a very well-regarded person asked me, "Does ISIS come from the Quran?" This is a very important person, a person who has the president's ear sometimes. And I'm just like, why are we talking about the Quran? Why are we not talking about Idiot King #1 who goes into a country under false pretenses and releases eighty thousand enemy soldiers into the hinterlands without pay? And then two years later is surprised and wondering why is there an insurgency? And then figures out a few years later how to put them back on payroll and calls it an Awakening? So suddenly now these people "woke up," because they're getting a check every week. So now there's no insurgency, because the guys who were insurgent are now on payroll, so they're fighting for us. So there's no insurgency, let's take them off payroll again. Now you've got an insurgency. So now put somebody in power who starts killing them all, Nouri al-Maliki starts killing them, and then you have a murderous insurgency. We destroy the Middle East, and then we wonder where this violence is coming from? We have to think for ourselves about all this.

ALI: There's an assumption that Muslims' relationship with their own religion is somehow static and in a vacuum, and that's not the case. As far as I know, talking about myself, my friends…we're struggling. We're struggling with our religion, and our consciousness of religion has been formed in a post-9/11 world. That has had a profound effect on how I understand my religion, how I respond to it, how I deal with it. To talk about the theological schisms, about what the debates are, assumes that there is one big debate, or one or two big debates. As much as it is a community struggle, it's very much a personal struggle as well.

VENUGOPAL: Give me an example.

ALI: I'm hesitant because I really dislike talking about the hijab, but I will.

When I was in college, for whatever reason, I became a bit more religious, and I decided I was going to wear a hijab. But I didn't. I thought about it for several weeks, and I just never did it because I thought I wouldn't feel comfortable, that it would just be a phase. Later on, I decided to write a piece about the hijab, and my mother's experience wearing the burqa in Pakistan. Six years later, now I've realized that this is a personal struggle with the hijab, with how I think about it, what my mother's relationship with the hijab has been. I made that public, which is not a bad thing, but I realize I did it under the pressure of having to explain what Muslims are. Or somehow having to define a woman's right to choose. In the West, we're just obsessed with jihad and hijab, and it's mind-numbing.

MOGHUL: Islam is a lot of different things. It's your heritage, it's your identity, it can be imposed on you, it can be chosen. I've met people in the United States who identify as just Muslim, culturally Muslim, secular Muslim, atheist Muslim, Sunni Muslim, Shia Muslim, but the simple fact is, this entire demographic, people are talking about deporting it. So it doesn't matter if you have a thousand differences, because there's a guy who literally, when asked to elaborate on his deportation proposal, was like, "Well, we'll just ask them, 'Are you Muslim?'" The TSA has made more people Muslim than anyone I know in the last fifty years; I don't care what your theology is, you're getting strip-searched if you're flying while Muslim. So there's Islam as your own identity, and then there's Islam that's imposed on you. And that is an interesting element of the modern Muslim experience I think Ayad is pointing to, that he's trying to write.

AKHBAR: Right. I'm writing from the particular to the universal.

AUDIENCE: You've all suggested that we're asking the wrong questions, thinking in the wrong way; I'm curious what questions you're grappling with right now, and what questions you think others should be grappling with?

MOGHUL: Racism or bigotry causes you to deny a group of people the complexity you allow yourself. So Bill Maher, for example, says Islam is the only religion that behaves like the Mafia. Which is really funny, because right now, and in the last fifty years, the United States has repeatedly funded governments that kill their critics. You know, freedom of speech. Funding the government of Saudi Arabia and militarily defending it, how many authors has our government killed? But it's okay, because we're secular and liberal and we had an Enlightenment. Our violence is excusable, because it's for national security.

The problem is that these defeated societies, militarily speaking, aren't institutionally complex. We can diffuse our responsibility across so many institutions that there's no one to blame. It's just the national security machine running in the background. When Obama said, "I didn't know that we were tapping Angela Merkel's phone," I'm afraid he *didn't* know. He probably didn't. This massively complex government is doing all these things that no one individual can get a handle on, so how do you respond when you are a society that's been invaded and crushed? You respond individually. What ISIS is doing is disgusting and terrible and vile, but what are we doing? Why don't we show the same ability to understand people's motivations? We can't understand why Muslims radicalize, although after San Bernardino the Republican party went even more nuts. But somehow we don't seem to understand that invading a country can lead to radicalization.

Ask whatever questions you want, but show the same level of complexity and sophistication. Rozina's comment was interesting. My mom wore a headscarf; she was one of seven sisters. My grandfather was a Sharia scholar going back several generations, and my mom was a radiation oncologist. He educated all of his daughters in the '50s and '60s. He didn't need Western modernity to be enlightened or rescued or saved, and he and many of his relatives, and my grandparents on my father's side as well, went to fight to save Europe from itself. And now they're barbarians.

VENUGOPAL: I saw you nodding along, Rozina.

ALI: Yeah, to Haroon's point about affording the other person complexity, too. What I love about this time right now is there are a lot more Muslim writers. I love that it's not so much that they're writing about Islam, but they're writing from the perspective of being a Muslim, or being a man, or being a woman, and that I think says more. That actually gets to: What is a person's experience? How do they perceive the world? And that gets closer to really understanding a Muslim, rather than somehow talking about Islam. Which is what I liked about Ayad's play, too. The point of art is to bring up questions.

AKHTAR: When I was a young student and had a teacher who changed my life and made me want to become a writer, she'd always say, "It's about questions, it's about questions," and I was like, "What are you talking about? Give me an answer." But then I had this sort of understanding. When I watch a game, when I watch the Packers, I want them to win, but I'm actually only truly engaged in the game when I'm not sure who's going to win. That's living in the question. The tension of the uncertainty is alive in that moment. When the game has been resolved, sure, I'm happy the Packers won, but I don't really care, because I'm going to go do something else now. That to me is about living in the question. That's what I think about.

AUDIENCE: I think that a lot of us who inhabit whatever strange, constantly changing Muslim identity we inhabit are faced with a sort of cumulative exhaustion. How can we manage that?

AKHTAR: I learned in high school that you can never define yourself by trying to be something opposite to what people say about you. If people say you're this thing, and your way of being is, "Oh, I'm *not* that thing," that pathway is inimical to self-knowledge. The discourse of Edward Said's *Orientalism,* as great as it is, is ultimately still about saying, This is what they say about us, we've gotta say we're not that thing. You can never know who you are when you define yourself in opposition to what other people say about you.

So for me, leading from that place of knowledge: I'm not searching to be something different from what other people say. You want to call me this that or the other? Great! I've got bigger fish to fry than what you're calling me. That becomes increasingly difficult and exhausting in an environment where people are coming at you with questions about what Islam means, and also Muslims who, frankly, are often enraged by some of the things I write. But I have to just lead the way with what interests me authentically.

VENUGOPAL: Haroon, you're a pundit now and then on TV, correct? You've been on Fox News, CNN. Why?

MOGHUL: Why. That's a great question.

AKHTAR: Because the Meem thing isn't working out too well.

MOGHUL: Ouch!

I was twenty-one, and I was elected president of the Islamic center at my university. It was my third day as president of the Islamic center, I was building an institution, and I got out of the subway Tuesday morning, and a plane hit the tower. For the next six to eight months, people would stick a microphone in my face: "Islam, jihad, Sharia, polygamy, answer!" I'm like, "Polygamy? I don't even have a girlfriend!" I mean, seriously? I actually tried talking to a Muslim girl on 9/11, because I was like, "Hey, we're all going to die now," and she's central Asian, and she's literally like, "Nobody knows I'm Muslim," and she walked away. Like, "You're on your own, homeboy."

I was thrust into that role. It's this professional Muslim identity that is exhausting, because you're trying to define your own relationship to Islam while you're constantly bombarded with questions. But if you don't do it, someone worse will. This is something that I say to Muslim communities all the time: It is not the case that if you do not create an answer to a problem, no one will—it's that someone worse will. If you don't find a mechanism by which to address the conflict in Syria, what people are feeling in Palestine, someone worse will present an answer. I forgot who the author was, but he said, "ISIS did not hijack our religion; they hijacked our grievances."

If you're constantly stuck in the oppositional mode, as Ayad pointed out, you're going to burn yourself out and nothing's going to be accomplished. At some point, you have to decide to go for broke and say, *This is what I believe, this is what I want to do.* If it's compelling and interesting, people will be engaged by it and shaped by it, but you kind of have to lead. There is a moral responsibility. There is a lot of ugliness in the Muslim world and in the name of Islam; I personally feel like that's an obligation on us to address, not least because, thanks to social media and so on and so forth, anyone anywhere can be recruited. And not only will they then potentially commit violence, but the ramifications, the repercussions, fall on that community, even if that community had no idea what was going to happen.

VENUGOPAL: In that role of being in front of the camera, in these highly reductive conversations, do you find yourself able to say, Yes, the Islamic world does have these problems, one two three, or do you find that's a dangerous thing to do?

MOGHUL: You have to own the problem at some level, if you work within communities and addressing issues. I mean, with Fox News, just don't get angry. It's amazing, you can say anything on Fox News as long as you don't get angry. They have no idea how to respond to that. You can say the most "outrageous" thing in a calm, level tone, like, "Well, you know, naturally, if you invade a country on false pretenses and kill tens of thousands of people, violence begets violence." And then they don't know what to do, because they want you to yell.

VENUGOPAL: In Arabic.

AKHTAR: I mean, this insane obsession with the literalism of the Second Amendment, case in point. It's the same kind of unthinking literalist, violent strain that people are alleging to find in Muslims' relationship to the Quran.

VENUGOPAL: Anything to add to that, either of you?

MOGHUL: I'm an historian of Islam in South Asia, and I would say look to the pre-modern: There were very few forced conversions. The Muslim model, militarily speaking, was very similar to the Roman. I'm not lauding this—it's medieval military expansion—but it was very much like the Roman: As long as you play by the rules, you enter the system. If you'd like to convert, that's great; if you don't, we're going to tax you. It wasn't a democracy, it wasn't a secular society, it was a pre-modern model. The best analogy is that if Obama was really a Muslim medievalist, he would invade Syria and kill Bashar al-Assad and marry his wife, and then their children would rule Syria. That's basically how it worked.

The challenge that you point to in 1947 is: What happens when a pre-modern society is forced into modernity? That's an ugly process. The partition of India is actually not very different from the creation of homogenous European societies. Ayad mentioned the French earlier on: You're French, you're French, that's it. Europe realized this ideal after World War II because these very homogenous societies were created, and now Europe is grappling again with diversity. There are more Muslims in Spain than Protestants. Why is that? Because the Protestants were wiped out. In the Muslim world it's the same thing. Now you're going to take power, what does it mean to take power, whom do you share power with? We all ask the same questions, and you have violent answers, you have nonviolent answers, you have exclusivist literalist answers, you have more sophisticated answers... The distortions come from the fact that you're trying to answer these questions at the same time that you're being attacked. And it's really hard for any colonial society; you see this in Chinese discourse all the time. How can we have these open conversations about who we are when we need to catch up to the West? And if we don't, we're going to be attacked again.

VENUGOPAL: Is there any reason to be hopeful for the next few years, the next generation?

AKHTAR: It's going to make a hell of a novel.

This transcript was adapted from a February 2016 conversation co-sponsored by PEN America and The Greene Space.

THE GREAT WALL

Eliot Weinberger

Richard Nixon, visiting the Great Wall of China in 1972, said: "I think you would have to conclude that this is a great wall."

Ronald Reagan, visiting the Wall in 1984, said: "What can you say, except it's awe-inspiring? It is one of the great wonders of the world." Asked if he would like to build his own Great Wall, Reagan drew a circle in the air and replied: "Around the White House."

Bill Clinton, visiting the Wall in 1998, said: "So if we had a couple of hours, we could walk ten kilometers, and we'd hit the steepest incline, and we'd all be in very good shape when we finished. Or we'd be finished. It was a good workout. It was great."

George W. Bush, visiting the Wall in 2002, signed the guestbook and said: "Let's go home." He made no other comments.

Barack Obama, visiting the Wall in 2009, said: "It's majestic. It's magical. It reminds you of the sweep of history, and that our time here on Earth is not that long, so we better make the best of it." During his visit, the Starbucks and KFC at the base of the Wall were closed.

THE WALL

Eliot Weinberger

1.

At 8:46 P.M. at Rudower Höhe, the sentry sneezed and a West Berlin customs officer shouted back, "Gesundheit!"

At 11:40 A.M. at the Kiesberg sentry post, three West Berlin youths shouted: "Hey guys, still smoking rags? Want an HB cigarette? Come over and get one."

At 9:25 A.M. at the Buckersberg sentry post, two men, aged thirty-five to forty, asked: "Did you see two children yesterday afternoon, riding their bicycles along the canal?" At 5:50 P.M., the fire department arrived and two divers went into the canal. At 6:50 P.M., they left, having found nothing.

At 12:19 P.M. at the Teltowkanal, a man about thirty years old called out: "I hope this shit ends soon, so we can be friends again."

At 1:15 p.m. at the Teltowkanal, three West Berlin policeman, drinking Coca Cola, asked, "Would you like one?"

At 3:30 P.M. at Forsthausallee, three women and a man called out to the sentry: "Can you shoot that crow? It's getting on our nerves."

At 10:00 P.M. at Heidekampgraben, a policeman asked: "Hi boys, are the mosquitoes bad over there too?"

At 8:40 A.M. at the Köllnische Heide sentry post, a girl about sixteen years old on the second story of the house at Wegastraße 36 removed her pullover and displayed her breasts. At 9:20 A.M. she put her pullover back on.

At 6:10 P.M. at Puderstraße, watchdog Trux bit through the fencing on the dog track and attacked a commander and his assistant on patrol. Twelve shots were fired and the dog died.

At 10:00 A.M. at Harzer Straße, a driver and a co-worker in a beer delivery van, registration B-CL 51, offered the sentries beer "if you come over."

At 15:59 P.M. at Lohmühlenstraße, a family in number 58/59 waved to a woman on the West Berlin side.

At 3:02 P.M. at Bahnhofstraße, a man in his mid-twenties said: "Go home and make yourself a cup of coffee."

At 7:05 P.M. at Kiefholzstraße, two girls, about fifteen years old, called to the sentry: "We love you! Come on over, we need something,"

At 1:30 P.M. at Bethaniendamm, a West Berlin customs official threw an empty lemonade bottle over the wall.

At 11:30 P.M. at Elsenstraße, three young women said: "Come on over, we've got the place to ourselves."

At 4:56 P.M. at Alexandrinenstraße, a man shouted at the sentries: "Have you really thought about it?"

At 3:12 P.M. at Checkpoint Charlie, an American soldier held up a 25 x 30 cm photo of a nude woman.

At 2:03 P.M. at Ackerstraße, a man on a viewing platform threw his hat over the wall.

At 5:13 P.M. at the Marschall Bridge, a female corpse was found in the water barricades.

At 12:20 A.M. at Nordgraben, two men shouted to the sentry post: "Say something!"

At 10:15 A.M. at Wolliner Straße, an old lady threw a bag of oranges over the wall.

At 1:13 A.M. at Korsörer Straße, two men threw a pack of cigarettes (brand Ernte 23) over the wall, saying "You can smoke these."

At 5:15 P.M. at Schulzestraße, a sixteen-year-old boy on the S-Bahn rail platform said: "I have a question. What time is it?"

2.

Border guard ▮▮▮▮▮▮▮▮▮▮▮ was commended for preventing a breach of the border with his watchdog Cella.

Border guard ▮▮▮▮▮▮▮▮▮▮▮ was commended for keeping his motorcycle in excellent condition.

Border guard ▮▮▮▮▮▮▮▮▮▮▮ was commended for his measured and exemplary appearance.

Border guard ▮▮▮▮▮▮▮▮▮▮▮ was commended for fulfilling military norms.

Border guard ▮▮▮▮▮▮▮▮▮▮▮ was commended for advocating the politics of the state in conversations with the other comrades in the barracks.

Border guard ▮▮▮▮▮▮▮▮▮▮▮ was commended for encouraging his comrades to achieve higher performances.

Border guard ▮▮▮▮▮▮▮▮▮▮▮ was commended for having his weapons locker win first place among all regiment lockers.

Border guard ▮▮▮▮▮▮▮▮▮▮▮ was commended for excellent performance as a member of the chemical group.

Border guard ███████████████ was commended for his correct actions.

Border guard ███████████████ was commended for his class-appropriate manner when faced with enemy provocation at the border.

3.

Border guard ███████████████ was censured for lacking ideological clarity.

Border guard ███████████████ was censured for sleeping in the watchtower.

Border guard ███████████████ was censured for telling a comrade that he would like to go to the West just one day to visit a brothel.

Border guard ███████████████ was censured for lackadaisically performing his early morning gymnastics and not bothering to touch his toes.

Border guard ███████████████ was censured for copying passages from Franz Kafka in his diary.

Border guard ███████████████ was censured for owning a toy Mercedes automobile with an integrated measuring tape.

Border guard ███████████████ was censured for being a committed fan of beat music.

Border guard ███████████████ was censured for falling prey to ideological diversion due to his religious convictions.

Border guard ███████████████ was censured for making shapes in the snow with his feet, out of boredom.

Border guard ███████████████ was censured for firing single shots instead of shooting in short bursts.

Border guard ██████████████ was censured for being afraid.

Border guard ██████████████ was censured for shooting his gun at such an angle that the border violator was not forced to stop.

Border guard ██████████████ was censured for committing suicide by hanging.

4.

January 28, 1969: Eighty shots were fired at possible border violator Manfred ██████████████ at Kremmener Straße, near the Friedrich-Ludwig-Jahn sports fields. None struck the target, but he was captured, interrogated by the State Security Police and turned over to a People's Police force car unit. He was discovered to be in a state of inebriation.

April 9, 1969: One hundred forty-eight shots from two watchtowers were fired at the border violator Johannes Lange of Dresden. Fire ceased when the border violator had been destroyed. All of the eight border guards received commendations and three were given a material bonus of a wristwatch.

February 2, 1969: Forty-eight shots were fired at an unknown border violator at the Massante Bridge who was carrying a 3.5-meter wooden plank, which he leaned against the wall and scurried up. His fate is unknown.

November 10, 1965: Seventeen shots were fired at border violator Heinz Cyrus ██████████████, a milkman from the island of Rügen. None struck the target. He fled into a building at Gartenstraße 85, ran up the stairs to the roof and attempted to hide by hanging from the gutter. The gutter collapsed, and he fell four stories and died in the People's Police Hospital (Scharnhorststraße) the following day.

November 11, 1969: Thirty-four shots were fired at Heinz-Jürgen ██████ ██████████, a fourteen-year-old, in the water under the Oberbaum Bridge. Earlier in the day, the boy had been questioned at Police Station

85 about a theft and was scared to go home. None of the shots struck the target, but the boy was apprehended by boat and arrested.

April 29, 1966: One hundred seventy-six shots were fired at Paul Stretz, a West Berliner who, in an advanced state of inebriation, had decided to go for a swim in the Spandau Shipping Canal, in East Berlin territory, and was mistaken for a border violator. Four of the shots struck the target, who was destroyed.

August 18, 1964: One fatal shot was fired by border guard ███████████ ████, age twenty, in the back of possible border violator Hildegard Trabant, age thirty-seven, of Tilsiter Straße. She was discovered hiding behind an elder bush beside abandoned railroad tracks at Schönhauser Allee, sixty meters from the border. Her personal effects, returned to her husband, a member of the People's Police force, were:

an identity card
Party card, membership No. 146,664
144.28 East German marks
1 key chain with keys
5 handkerchiefs
1 pair of shoes
1 blue slip
1 pair of stockings
1 dress suit
1 bottle of perfume
1 pair of sunglasses
1 pair of eyeglasses
1 nail clippers
1 comb
12 cigarettes (Jubilar brand)
1 pen
1 notebook
1 postcard, sent September 12, 1963, from a relative in Recklinghausen
1 package of tampons (Neo brand)

SAMIYA SCHMIDT

Antoine Volodine

TRANSLATED BY JEFFREY ZUCKERMAN

The night is long. Very turbulent, very strange, and very long. Samiya Schmidt takes on her furious form. Then she escapes all standards. Neither Solovyei with his very considerable powers nor, obviously, Morgovian is able to calm her down.

She is covered in very hard scales.

She lands terrible blows.

She moves at an incredible speed.

She transforms her scream into energy.

She no longer has blood, or rather she no longer has either blood or the absence of blood.

She is neither dead nor alive, nor in dreams nor in reality, nor in space nor in the absence of space. She makes theater.

She allies with the fuel.

She starts fires of cold flames.

She allies with the void, with the controlled fuel, with the suspect fuel, with the demented and uncontrollable fuel.

She comes and goes at full speed between the two cores, between the well that the Gramma Udgul watches and the emergency reactor cobbled together beneath the Soviet.

She pronounces curses, prayers to forces, to the forces she knows, to the forces she has heard of, and to the forces that don't exist.

She runs in the darkness faster than a bullet. She runs in the night forest. She goes beneath the larches to the old forest and then she comes back. Several times she goes around the Levanidovo, running along the border of black trees. She comes back to the nuclear crackles, she draws circles around the nuclear cores until the oil in the pumps catches fire, she traces circles until the icy flames thunder and twirl around the fuel rods.

She enumerates the crimes of her father and she orders the supernatural forces to bring her father back to the region of the camps, to force him to stay within a nest of barbed wires, in a harsh regime's confines.

She doesn't meet anyone, or rather she refuses to look at those in her way, whether they do or don't belong to the horde of the living, to the cohort of dogs, or to the infinite herd of the dead.

She covers herself in hard and rustling scales.

She covers herself in black droplets.

She covers herself in sparks.

Her hair briefly grows back and grows down to her ankles, then once again her scalp is bald.

She makes wind, she makes theater, she makes black sky, she makes four black heavens.

She calls the forces when she is against the forest, she calls the forces when she sees around her the earth of the tunnels, she calls the forces once she is close to the fuel rods.

She goes to the beginning of time and she blows with a yell, then she reaches the end of time and she blows.

She appeals to the former leaders of the world revolution, she appeals to the great figures, the anonymous masses, the disappeared peoples.

In reciting compact lists, reduced to a short piercing babble, she appeals to the heroes of the First and Second Soviet Union, those she knows and those she just invented, the major and minor scholars, the inflexible proletarians, the engineers, the veterinarians, the archivists who have already left their contribution to the spinning worlds, the sacrificial liquidators who gave their lives to the molten nuclear sites, the heroic detainees and soldiers, the heroic musicians, the cosmonauts.

When she comes back to the boiler room, facing Solovyei, she knocks him over and pummels him, she asks him why he isn't dead, and, when he defends himself, she slaps him with her hands harder than iron and she asks him to stop going into her like an object without thoughts, and she pummels him furiously.

She also asks him to stop going into her sisters like lands of inert flesh, without thoughts or sensitivity to heat and cold.

She makes the cold flames and the warm flames burst from Solovyei's body when she touches him.

She beats him, she asks him to stop his worthless immortality and to no longer inflict such worthless immortality on those surrounding him.

In order to humiliate her father, she prevents him from replying to the hailstorm of blows she lands.

She crosses the Levanidovo in every direction, she goes through walls unharmed, like neutrinos passing through the Earth without destroying the Earth or themselves.

She forces Solovyei to run behind her to keep her from setting fire to the village and to put out the blazes she lights, she hears him panting behind her and sometimes she makes a sudden volte-face to bang into him, knock him over, and curse him.

She covers herself in a soot that neither fades away nor crackles, and suddenly she is radiantly beautiful, then again she looks like a free-running dark creature.

She goes from the Soviet boiler room to the Gramma Udgul's workshop, she slips down the well to the core's heart in the shadowy depths, she goes back up after having touched the heart, she runs again at high speed to the center of the village, she goes past her house, past her room, she doesn't look at herself in the mirror, she goes down the stairs, she comes back to the boiler room, she hits the pipes, the pumps, the doors illogically distributed throughout the jumble of burning pipes, she goes to Solovyei's nest and, when he's in her way, she pummels him.

She flies under the ground as well as above it and sometimes she speeds so quickly she is neither here nor there.

She never touches Vassilissa Marachvili's remains.

She never contemplates or examines Vassilissa Marachvili's body.

She crosses the curtains of flames shuddering on the wall of the reactor, she moves over Vassilissa Marachvili's cadaver, but she doesn't contemplate her or examine her in passing.

She doesn't consider any of the Gramma Udgul's complaints as she exhorts her to calm down and accept her fate, accept the mutations that have seized hold of her but guarantee her endless existence within the Levanidovo, which encourage her again and again to accept the deathless life granted by her father, to accept her father's monstrosities, to accept her father as he is.

She covers herself with specks of cutting ice.

She covers herself with night.

She makes blinding night, she makes immobile tempests, she makes theater, she makes breaths, she makes sky, she makes twelve black heavens.

She summons exceptional tribunals to judge Solovyei.

She covers herself in a dull plumage.

She covers herself in a black, urticant down.

She makes ink-black, she makes theater, she makes blizzard, she makes tar-black, she makes the thousandth stinking category.

When Solovyei transmits through the loudspeakers his dreadful digressionary poems in order to cover the clamors coming out of his daughter's mouth, she traces spirals around the loudspeakers while reciting extracts from epic literature that she knows by heart, or fundamental accusations against her father.

She assembles a popular tribunal, she forms a jury of incorruptible Chekists, Red Army soldiers, Second Soviet Union avengers, exemplary zeks, model detainees.

She accuses her father of the manipulation and sorcery of deceased humans and of being proud of it.

She accuses him of vileness and incestuous relations with imaginary daughters, with real, dead, or imaginary spouses, she accuses him of debauchery committed against willing victims, of fornicating with the Gramma Udgul, she also accuses him of having done rut with his own daughters, with a list of girls whose names she says one by one, all without any end to her coming and going down the village's streets and tunnels, with the girls whose names she says at random into the darkness, with unknown women whose names she invents, with girls like Solayane Mercurin, Imiriya Good, Nadiyane Beck, Keti Birobidjan, Maria Djibil, Maria Dongfang, Lulli Grünewald, Barbara Rock, with kolkhozniks lost to memory, with poetesses whose names and faces and poems weren't left to posterity, with the female communist prisoners locked up with him in camps, with counterrevolutionary women and representatives of the first, the second, and the third stinking category, and, to end the list, she accuses him once more of having had ignominious relations with his own daughters.

She accuses him of genetic crimes.

She crosses the Levanidovo while spreading insane rumors and painful childhood memories.

She claims that she isn't even born to an unknown mother, she says that she wasn't born, she covers herself in a tarry mist.

She covers herself in shining dust, she covers herself in shimmering points.

She covers herself in animal-hide straps, she covers herself in frost, she keeps crossing the roads and the tunnels of the Levanidovo with such a speed that nobody witnesses her passage.

She makes poison, she makes hurricane, she makes theater.

Suddenly she is vertiginously radiant, suddenly she sparkles, and almost immediately she is a handful of magical flesh that runs and runs in the countryside and slams into tree trunks, walls of farms where all the animals are dead, Morgovian when he stupidly appears in her path.

She tears Morgovian, she tears his old peasant-husband's clothes, she slashes Morgovian, she destroys his backward body, kept deceptively alive by Solovyei's powers, she takes those spells out of his body, she tries to kill Morgovian when he comes between her and the Soviet reactor, every time she tries to kill him.

She bangs the pipes until the metal sings.

She covers herself in the fur of a white she-wolf, and at that moment once again she looks like a lost young girl from the Cultural Revolution, fragile in her unisex military uniform, her only vanity a red ribbon at the end of her braids and a red badge on her shapeless green cap, and then she resumes her frantic race through the night's flames.

She hits the fuel rods, she wields them, she shakes the vessel water, she can't keep going out of despair, she hurls herself against the silent walls, and on them she leaves traces of soot and despair, she beats the vessel water, she bounces back and forth from channel to conduit, she bounces with fleshy noises against the walls, with clanking noises, with avalanching noises.

She makes revenge, she makes depth, she makes darkness, she makes theater.

She reads a long-winded accusation, she accuses Solovyei of counterrevolutionary immortality, she reproaches him for his habit of illegally penetrating the dreams of his daughters in order to transmit an excess of immortality that they don't care about.

She beats her father, she hits his memory, she dirties his memory as he dirtied the memory of all those he penetrated in order to keep them in a false state, between life and death, she accuses her father of orchestrating the Levanidovo like a revolting dream, of orchestrating the forest, of orchestrating the steppes, and of the concentrational hereafter of the camps, she accuses him for imprisoning within himself all the living and the dead of the Levanidovo and his hereafter.

In front of the popular tribunal, she denounces Solovyei's suspected ubiquity, his affiliations with several stinking categories at the same time, his poor management of the Radiant Terminus kolkhoz, his criminal ways of sourcing provisions, she accuses him of assassinating merchants in the forest, she accuses him of pillaging the caravans, she denounces Solovyei's terrifying stare, his appearance of a triumphant kulak, his magic axes, his lust.

She makes theater, she makes opera, she makes cantopera.

She causes serious damage in the places she passes through and over the bodies she pummels.

Compacting the flood of words as much as possible, she recites in their entirety the Marxist-Leninist brochures talking about the world revolution, the end of history and the joys awaiting the generations to come, the user's guides for fuel cells, hygiene manuals for kolkhozniks, the post-exotic romances of her childhood, the feminist manifestos for women neither living nor dead, the treatises on practical oncology, the booklets for pig breeders, yak farmers, beekeepers, teachers put in extreme pedagogical conditions, adventure novels set in the Great North.

She hangs from the pipes in which pressurized vapor hisses, she breaks doors, she throws planks behind her, wood shavings, she throws iron plates over her shoulder, locks still surrounded within the meat of doors, she speeds through the night and through walls, vessels, boiling circuits, then she comes back toward Morgovian and she beats him, she heads toward Solovyei once again and she pummels him.

She feeds her impotent rage only images and speed.

She covers herself in strips of flesh, metallic excrescences, organic vapors, and a second later she's already dressed anew in armor of unbelievably hard and rustling scales.

She keeps racing back and forth across the Levanidovo, along its surface and underground.

She makes lightning, she makes bolts, she runs, she imagines that she is dressed entirely in fire and blood.

Then suddenly nobody knows where she is.

She makes silence.

She makes theater in the sudden silence.

She makes absence.

She has disappeared and she is silent.

MAUREEN

Sara Majka

Or another Portland story, one of those heard and almost forgotten, told late at night, when no one has anywhere to be and you're not sure if anyone is talking. Maureen had been the bartender at the Regency Bar for nearly twenty years. The place was under the highway ramp and had dark wood, torn covers in the booths, and old lamps, though it wasn't lovely in the way this might suggest, just generic. Most of the men drank Bud from bottles and sat for a long time, and sometimes, on slow nights, Maureen would lean over and talk to them. She had been beautiful when she started, and most of the men could remember that. One night she told them about being at the beach with the man she had once been married to and their baby daughter. It was easy to see a younger Maureen on the shore, wearing a stretched-out bathing suit and cutoffs, her long hair greasy but shining. Already some of the weight gained, but it would have looked good on her. There would have been something sympathetic in the thickening under her arms. And her husband, thin and bare-chested, a mustached man spread across the blanket, with their baby playing in between. The two of them drinking cups of beer, and afterward walking barefoot through the parking lot, teetering on pavement embedded with small rocks. The shock of the hot car, then lifting the baby in and buckling her, careful not to clip the fat of her legs.

The baby had died later, a few years later, in a car accident. Maureen had been newly divorced when it happened. She had just moved into the apartment and her ex came on Saturdays to pick up the girl, Clarice. That morning Maureen could tell he had been drinking, but still, she helped her daughter into her coat and went back upstairs. She enjoyed the empty apartment. She would do nothing—pick up laundry, smoke a cigarette, take a bath. She had been lying in bed, watching the curtain, smelling her shoulder, when the phone rang.

After that time, she felt there was something wrong with her, that she was empty in ways she shouldn't have been. That emptiness prepared her for what she saw on the town green one day, years later—a little girl who looked like her daughter, in a group with other children, being led down a path. She looked to see if anyone else noticed, thinking perhaps they were an imaginary thing that had come to fill the space. But other people, too, saw the children.

The next time, she followed them to story time at the library. She stood outside the children's room in the basement, watching the kids, then went to the information desk and asked if she could read. Well, the woman said, it's usually the librarian or someone at the senior center, but we always like help here. So on Tuesdays she put on her good dress, a thin spring dress she had owned for years, and brushed her hair while watching the old man in the garden out her window, the old man working his tomato patch in a green hat, moving over the earth like a delicate animal. She didn't look at him when she backed out of the drive, but felt he knew.

Afterward, after reading at the library, she would smoke by the fence and try not to get too close to what was happening. She felt if she moved smoothly enough, without sharpness or rise in her voice, if she didn't pay attention, or look closely, only watched from the corner of her eyes… The few times she approached the girl were an allowance. Did you like that book? she had asked her. What she must have seemed to the little girl, with her off voice and stifled inconsistency. She wasn't in control, but felt if she moved slowly, almost crept, that nothing would startle and break loose.

When her ex-husband appeared at her door one day, she thought it was a harbinger, the very thing she was trying to avoid. It reminded her of the Saturdays when he had picked up their daughter. Opening the door was like that, too, except he was older and it hadn't done well for him. It was as if they had agreed on this play, but their aging and lack of reason made it a pitiful thing. She looked past him to see if the man was in the garden, but she didn't see him. What do you want? she asked her ex-husband. He held up his hands. Just to talk to you. She asked him to wait while she put on shoes. Upstairs she tied her raincoat, put on flats. She looked out the bathroom window for the old man but still didn't see him and wondered if that was a bad omen.

They walked to the corner bar, slipping inside the door. They stood near each other. It was midday and nearly empty. He was more lost than she was. It occurred to her that he was drunk, but she couldn't tell. Do you still drink the same? she asked. He offered to get it, but she thought he might not have money, and said, No, I'll get it, find us a seat. He picked a booth along the side wall; tinted windows showed a yellowed version of the empty street. She bought one drink and sat at the edge of the seat, sliding it to him.

I'm sorry, he said. I didn't think of what I would say. He wrapped his hands around the glass. Instead of looking at his face, she looked outside. It was raining, what looked like yellow rain on a darker yellow sidewalk. I'm getting married again, he said. We're going to move to Florida. I'm going to start up a bar there. He waited for her to say something. She said that she had to go. He reached for her, but she slid from the booth.

On the sidewalk, she put a hand in her purse and fumbled with her cigarettes. She lit one, threw it down, walked back to the bar. She stood in the entryway. There was a man in the far booth where they had been. He was tall, lanky, dark-haired. She took steps toward him, but his features aligned into those of a stranger's.

During her shifts she often smoked to steady herself. You could see her out there, holding her sweater closed with one arm and turning away from the wind. She looked like those women you find in rural areas who have kids, do the cooking, and work, who have no femininity in them, but also nothing hard, it was just that life had brought them to having no extra gestures.

LUKIN'S BED

Vivian Abenshushan

TRANSLATED BY SUSAN OURIOU

At one point or another, each of us found ourselves alone and we all ended up heading for Lukin's bed. He assured us we would found a new civilization, the civilization of the bed, shared by millions of men, a civilization that would eventually blanket the globe. It was obviously nothing but a fantasy—who could get enthusiastic about a world inhabited by such a cold, hopeless lineage as ours? I think Lukin was trying to do right by us, to be a friend and comfort us like any good host would. Moreover, he didn't want to see us leave since he, too, had been forsaken, sad, and free. But in a certain sense his prophecy was being fulfilled: Soon Lukin's bed—a king-size one that used to belong to his ex-wife Sonia's great-grandparents—proved insufficient. It was then that our hard-working, fraternal community of abandoned men began building The Bed.

This all took place during the famous season of mass divorces. It was wintertime and the ice-cold nights in the city were unbearable without a companion. What to do? Where to go? How to put a stop to the stampede? From one minute to the next, women had felt the call to flee and a huge hubbub started up in the streets: Hundreds of movers and moving vans came and went with books and plants and stools and all the carved wooden or ceramic figurines that had sparked little interest in us beforehand, but which, deep down, were so familiar. But our spouses wanted more convincing responses, an "Ah!," an "Oh!," a "How extraordinary our conjugal blanket, our brass ashtray, the grime on our walls is!"—something to give our home its own unrelinquishable character. I believe the women's demands, the slight pressure they brought to bear on us, were not the result of a mere caprice; they were more like desperate measures driven by the women's anticipation of their imminent flight, as though they had to convince themselves that neither they nor their belongings were just passing through our lives and that we, their provisional husbands, would love them even after they were gone. How difficult it must have been, now that I think about it, to lead such an unsettled life, forever going from one spouse to the next, from one city to the next, like gypsies carrying their bedrolls on their backs.

It goes without saying that in this high-altitude mountain city the change in seasons is so dramatic that the climate mutates brutally—not only do the trees lose their leaves and the birds migrate in flocks, but our partners, like nature, begin to move, one being exchanged for another, along with the contents of our homes, which were obliged to adopt a totally new look, integrating objects brought by the new female companions, who always arrive loaded down with used items, each one bearing its own weight and scratches from the past. Making room for them is obviously not as simple as all that, and loving them as one's own even less so (the objects, I mean). Some women, especially the foreign ones or the beautiful, intellectual local women, who after setting out for new horizons, brazenly make their way back to us—thus accelerating the natural divorce process. Here, in this progressive high-altitude mountain city, it has been decades since the menfolk have been able or, in fact, have wanted to sire offspring. If we do on certain occasions agree to live with foreign children—one way of putting it—it's mostly because instinctively we know it won't last.

Still, no one knows what provokes the stampedes or whether they will stop one day. In the grip of some irrepressible impulse, the women simply leave shortly before the first snowfall, without a word as to why or where they're going, leaving us gaping, incredulous, stunned. Every year the same scene plays out and every year our expression is the same, as though past experience has taught us nothing or, frankly, that we enjoy suffering. What's left to us? The litany we comfort each other with, "No matter, old pal, it's just a passing fancy, they'll soon get over it." Such ingeniousness! One could ask oneself, as our ingenious friend Lukin has been doing for decades: If we've renounced without the slightest remorse or pain all hope of having children, why haven't we grown accustomed to celibacy? The way Lukin tells it, such emotional autonomy represents something like a "leap of civilization," namely the acquisition of absolute freedom in the face of nature's pressure. However, that supposedly glorious phase of our evolution has yet to take place. Something quite to the contrary has, in fact, transpired: Our restlessness and dependency have only increased. As well as the severity of our insomnia. Each time the snow begins to fall on the mountain, we hold tight to the notion that this is it, that this will be the last lonely winter, that there will be no more mass flights, that the next batch of women will provide us with lasting serenity (until death or beyond), giving us enough time and opportunity to better understand them, their little obsessions, their whims, and to love them extravagantly, both them and their rare objects, such as my ex-spouse Francisca's small Tuscan table, which I thought slightly vulgar at first, but which now is the bearer of so many wonderful memories that I feel incapable of ever getting rid of it.

The fact is, far from decreasing, the number of divorces has multiplied and the diaspora of women has become increasingly unpredictable. Last winter was one of the worst ever, unforgivably cruel. Never before had every single woman left, absolutely everyone, all together at the same time; previously, at least ten or twenty used to stay through the year, either because they lacked the energy to take flight or because they were entirely satisfied with their husbands. What's more, we always used to be able to turn to the comfort of the girls in the brothel run by Mikaína—an extraordinary woman with huge hips whose statue presides over the small square in the middle of our city's central plaza. The girls only ever abandoned their posts after our ex-wives' replacements had arrived during the rainy season. This was a small gesture from Mikaína toward her clients, for which we gave thanks and then some, sponsoring the aforementioned square that bears her name. But in last winter's stampede, even they left. How sad to come home from work only to find half-empty houses! As though during the morning a gang of invisible thieves had burglarized even the most remote corners of the city without making a sound.

General consternation ensued, if not something verging on panic. I, for instance, sat staring at my hands for hours at a time without knowing what to do with them. I kept asking myself, "Where on Earth shall I put them now?" I was so used to placing them gently on Francisca's back right next to the nape of her neck as we slept that, the first night in her absence, I was obliged to lie on my back with my arms stretched out in front of me like a sleepwalker. But that was nothing compared to the shivering brought on by the cold. Shortly before dawn when the city hit the freezing mark, it felt to me—and at the same time to all my fellow citizens, I know—that we would never survive without our wives. An insidious, freezing wind squeezed through the cracks in the doors and windows to penetrate our bones like the sharp tips of icebergs, setting us to trembling uncontrollably, the victims of stomach cramps and unspeakable anguish. From my alcove, I could hear the comings and goings of my neighbors who, stiff with cold like me, were unable to keep to their beds. In order not to freeze to death, one had to get to one's feet and pace among old, lusterless pieces of furniture like rats that come out at night.

We all knew full well that the sessions of wandering would invariably end in bitter weeping or pointless pleas. But we tried to keep it to ourselves. In the morning, when my buddies and I met at the market or the Laundromat, we laughed and slapped each other on the back to ease our dejection. "They'll be back," we told each other. No one seemed to be starving or ill, since we mountain men had learned a century ago how to cook even better than women and take care of ourselves. However, if we bothered to look a bit closer, the ravages of a bad night's sleep could not be concealed: sunken eyes surrounded by an ashen halo, pallid features, bad temper, and the oh-so-telling way of letting our words trail off at the end of a sentence. Most depressing of all was to see how insomnia had aggravated character flaws which, under normal circumstances, went unnoticed. My friend Umbertico, who owned the antiquarian bookstore in the center of town, stuttered more than usual; Antonín's armpits smelled worse than ever before; and Lukin, who loved nothing more than a good political harangue, went on and on spouting nonsense. For my part, I existed in a constant state of melancholy and stupor, with the sensation that everything around me took place in maddeningly slow motion.

Unfortunately, this was not just an impression: The slightest gesture, the slightest activity no matter how mundane, took us twice the time it used to; for instance, we had to be sure to ask for the bill as soon as we placed our order for breakfast at the restaurant if we didn't want to still be there at suppertime. But it wasn't the general lack of sleep and intense cold that contributed to the mood of sluggishness and lethargy. The principal cause was to be found in the women's absence: Without them, our obligations and work multiplied to the point of exhaustion, any hours of effective rest disappeared, and the economy entered into alarming recession, as though money itself were trudging through mounds of snow. In those strange, incomprehensible days, the life of our modern high-altitude mountain city adopted a nineteenth-century pace, with letters taking three months to reach their destinations and physicians losing their patients en route! We felt insecure, prone to mistakes, and backward in the eyes of the world.

At times like these, Lukin and his theories sprang into action, although, for him, action consisted of nothing more than a never-ending tongue-wagging. "Hope," he declared to the regulars at Miguel's canteen, "is the most refined of delaying tactics." He liked to reiterate, oblivious to the fact we were sick of hearing it, that as long as we failed to endure with dignity both the nights and the snowfalls and continued to expect anything at all from the women, our emancipation would be postponed indefinitely. Hadn't we taken care of ourselves for all these years? Yet we continued to suffer from the women's tyranny and the desire to see them return home. The way Lukin put it, our history, our economy, our progressive high-altitude mountain civilization, were forever undermining in the wintertime all that was achieved in the summer, which was why we hit a point of stagnation every year. Everyone knows how hard it is to get over a divorce; not only does one's self-confidence suffer and one's will falter, one is also obliged to start over from scratch and fertilize unknown terrain again and again, like a poor directionless nomad. What could be expected of a city suffering from mass divorce? Paralysis. But things didn't have to be this way...

One day as I was taking out the garbage, I bumped into Lukin coming up the stairwell of my building. He was running up quickly as though bringing me urgent news. He said, "Yesterday, the last women left. Victoria, the tavernkeeper's wife, and even Mikaína, who's taken all the girls from the brothel with her. Antonín's wife threw her things out the window and locked the apartment with a master key. Which she then swallowed. So Antonín had to spend the night at my place."

"We're done for," I said.

"No," he exclaimed in his usual booming leader's voice, "we'll show them we have no need of them. Never again will we toss and turn between our sheets, stiff with cold!"

"You're repeating yourself," I said, looking him up and down.

"It doesn't matter."

"It does matter, Lukin. You're always repeating yourself, which is why Sonia left you."

"What I mean is that from now on, we can sleep together and continue our lives without them."

"Fine," I said with little conviction.

Lukin invited me to spend the night in his apartment along with Antonín. Armed with my pillow and a change of clothes, I arrived before the appointed hour, since the sun had set early and my apartment, stripped of curtains and carpets, was an icebox now. Worse than the cold, however, was the silence. Scarcely three weeks ago, I would make maté or tea with butter for Francisca and myself when we returned home from work shortly after sunset. We'd talk effortlessly, at ease, as if for a moment life had lost all its rancor and become simple and pleasing. But when Francisca left, all conversation left, too. What's more, because of my solitude, the air in my apartment began to acquire a vinegary, caged animal smell that thoroughly discouraged me. That same smell now permeated Lukin's house and Umbertico's bookstore and Miguel's tavern. The entire city smelled rank, and there was no woman's scent making it possible to distinguish one spot from another like before. Everything was the same, monotonous, humdrum. Why go to Miguel's tavern, for instance, if all one found there was Lukin and Umbertico and Antonín? But life was so tough after a divorce that anything, even Lukin's repetitions and Antonín's stench, seemed less oppressive than my own silence.

Since it was Friday, Umbertico, Miguel, and two other friends, Pedro and Jonás—unemployed due to our economy's winter paralysis—showed up at Lukin's apartment. They looked awful. To comfort them, Lukin welcomed them with an exquisite spaghetti alla puttanesca; after tapping the side of a glass a couple of times with his spoon, he announced, "Tonight we won't look at photographs or, worse yet, share secrets about our women..."

He was referring, of course, to our traditional exchange of pictures—a countless unfurling of images of the women who had crossed our paths—which for decades animated our get-togethers every Friday at Lukin's house. It's true that the relaxed sessions were wonderful (and indispensable during months of abstinence), since we not only played darts, but could gaze at the wives of our friends, prying further into their virtues and flaws, for instance, and a few more private tidbits concerning their favorite books and sexual fantasies, realizing there was a good chance we'd find the next woman to share our bed among their ranks (such was our destiny). Since the women in question were distant in both time and space, it was almost possible to see them as mere abstractions; any one of us could desire his neighbor's wife without remorse. It's no wonder then that Lukin's announcement elicited a protest from Antonín: "Without the pictures, these get-togethers are just plain absurd."

"The only thing that's absurd," Lukin snapped, "is to keep living under this horrible yoke, the yoke of hope... I hate seeing you turn into beggars on life's road every year. The women won't be back! We shouldn't let them back! Think about it, my friends, be reasonable: Why humiliate ourselves before them any longer? We've conquered the pressures of the species, we've managed to stifle the impulse toward conception. So let's take advantage of the opportunity and liberate ourselves from all suffering and all unhealthy passion, too: jealousy, imaginary fears, infidelity. Let's not waste another night thinking about them! At least here in this apartment where you have always been welcome, let us never again worship women... I'm sorry Antonín, but if you don't agree, you have the option of going home."

Since Lukin had always been a host beyond reproach, his intransigence made us suspect that he had something up his sleeve. From then on, he was spared our reproaches—if only to avoid having him launch into another exhausting harangue on men's liberation and the leap of civilization. After several weeks of bad nights, our brains dulled, our nerves hanging by a thread, Lukin's speeches could be hell. Antonín wisely held his tongue, too, not just because he no longer had a home to return to, but basically because he was fully absorbed in his spaghetti. From then on, we kept our wives to ourselves; however, every time Lukin went to the kitchen for bread or wine, Jonás would pull a picture out of his wallet to exchange with me under the table, the way boys trade collector's stamps, hiding them from their teacher's gaze. Soon enough, Lukin caught us in the act and, as he uncorked the fifth bottle of the night, said, "Let me see that picture."

I handed it over to general laughter. The picture was of Sonia, his ex-wife, who had also been Jonás's first, unforgettable love and Miguel's fourth, infernal spouse.

"The bitches," muttered Lukin under his breath. "The best thing for this city's future would be to throw these pictures into the fire, erasing all trace of their treacherous existence. But why not start right now? Come on, into the stove with them!"

"Yes!" cried Pedro; alcohol always went straight to his head. "Into the stove with them!"

Caught up in the sudden, irrational enthusiasm, Miguel and Jonás ran to the kitchen as well, ready to be done with their spouses once and for all; suffering from mortal exhaustion, both Antonín and I decided to leave the group and go to Lukin's bed to sleep. What better solution, we thought, than to put the wine's effects to good use conquering insomnia.

The next morning I awoke refreshed in body and clear of mind. I had slept perfectly; one could almost say I'd been transformed. For the first time since my separation, night hadn't brought its usual attacks of irrational fear. I found Lukin and Antonín in the kitchen, both men rosy-cheeked and eating breakfast without the slightest sign of insomnia or a hangover. What had once been Sonia's great-grandparents' king-size bed seemed to have injected us with a transfusion of life force.

Although there was little trace of our evening get-together, I did catch sight of a few of the pictures' remains on the floor: eyes, charred calves, and unidentifiable women's feet like the disfigured corpses that show up at the morgue, as though my friends had actually carbonized all memory of the women.

That afternoon I returned home to pack another bag, this time with the whole contents of my wardrobe. I didn't see it as an abuse of hospitality: I knew Lukin would gladly host me all winter without objection. On my way to his place, I stopped in a small shop to buy tea, eggs, and butter. I could hardly wait for dinner, knowing that afterward I would be able to stretch out on the soft, quilted bed next to my two best friends.

What a surprise on my arrival to be confronted with an entire army of abandoned men—Umbertico, Jonás, Miguel, Pedro, and a dozen other individuals, some unknown to me, some buddies I hadn't seen in decades—sitting around the hearth in which a fire burned with almost as much fervor as their discussion. At first I thought Lukin was hosting a huge dinner party, but soon I realized the purpose of the gathering was quite different: All the men present were throwing photograph after photograph of their spouses into the fire, talking exaltedly of "the next steps." Undoubtedly the first signs of an insurrection.

"Where's Lukin?" I asked, disconcerted.

"Building The Bed," they replied in unison.

I hurried over to the middle room, from which hammering could be heard. I found Lukin and Antonín furiously engaged in a ridiculous, haphazard effort: trying to make two beds into one. How? By roughly nailing their sides together, with a board to cover the small gap between them.

"What's all this about?" I asked indignantly, as though taking someone to task in my own home.

"It's all for our cause," Antonín rejoined. "Since the three of us slept as soundly as we did, maybe others will, too. We have to stick together, lend a helping hand. It's our only chance of getting out from under the women for good."

The speed with which Lukin had indoctrinated my friend was extraordinary. I left the room determined to retrieve my suitcase and return home, since I was positive I couldn't bear to spend a night with these men in the transports of spite. However, before I had time to reach the door, something incomprehensible and astounding happened: My own bed was making its way in just as I was about to make my way out. I recognized it immediately because of its salmon color, identical to the Tuscan bedside table, the color Francisca had painted it when she moved in with me.

"Would someone please tell me what my bed is doing here?"

The assembled men froze on the spot. Each one turned to look at me in a weighty silence full of reproach until one of the big men carrying my bed said, "Sorry, sir, but since you weren't home, we had to knock down your front door to get at the bed."

"Who in hell asked you to do any such thing?"

"I did," said Lukin, peering into the bedroom, hammer in hand. "We need to accommodate all these fine friends somehow and I didn't think you would refuse us the loan of your bed, given that I loaned you mine."

I felt consumed by shame, and in public no less. I let my suitcase drop and threw myself into the cause. What else could I do? I was as alone as they were.

In no time, Jonás's and Pedro's beds arrived—both in dubious taste—

as well as the beds belonging to a few other friends whose names I've forgotten. Also: several crates of wine from Miguel's tavern, a vast selection of adventure books donated by Umbertico, blankets, pillows, bags of rice and bread, first-aid kits, and several sacks of pictures that kept the fire going in the hearth. Each man brought what he could, and so, in less than four hours, Lukin's apartment had been transformed into a compact shelter for men about to take the reins of their lives back into their own hands. I couldn't say whether the scene was touching or pathetic, but the fact remains that we felt invincible.

As daybreak neared, the first set of beds had been assembled (stretching so far that they barely fit in the room and had to cut across it diagonally), and we prepared to rest. In all honesty, I was doubtful about the effectiveness of the set-up, which brought to mind with odious persistency the image of seven dwarves all sleeping in a row. However, we overcame the inconvenience of tight quarters by coming up with a few rules so as not to disturb each other as we slept: individual quilts, no water before bed, freedom of movement within a two-square-meter radius.

Today I still have trouble believing it, but perfect harmony reigned that night. I would even venture to say, without fear of exaggeration, that in twenty years of successive marriages, I had never known such gentleness, such an easy coming together. Especially in bed, so often the locus of struggles.

The conclusion we drew was that women were troublemakers and we were better off without them. Over the week, the number of blustering, hard-working men carrying furniture and wood back and forth grew by the minute. Their desire: to build a universal bed. In accordance with *The Inaugural Call to The Bed* drawn up by Lukin while he sat by the burning hearth, the community bed would eventually encircle the globe and be shared by millions of men. Each time I heard his words, it felt like The Bed was in fact an abstraction, a symbolic object, something like a statue representing the conquest of our freedom. However, all the effort expended to join headboards and bedframes convinced me that not only was Lukin serious, but for the first time in his life, he'd made the leap from theory to action.

No obstacle stood in the way of The Bed's advance: If the room wasn't spacious enough, walls were knocked down, an adjoining apartment was invaded, warehouses were purchased to house the fragments of the infinite cot. What's more, men in the neighboring building also banded together and began assembling their own Bed, as did men in neighboring districts, in the outlying areas of the city, and so on. The grand social movement consisted of wildly reproducing cells.

The days were full of activity. We had recovered our tarnished virility, the shine had returned to our camaraderie. But it didn't stop there: During the construction of communal beds, our city lived under the ascending signs of a buoyant economy. Soon we began to believe that Lukin should become our great leader.

One night, however, I noticed Lukin wasn't in our bed. I reached out with my right arm several times, disturbing his covers, finding nothing but an empty hollow. That was when I began to hear giggling and moans coming from the living room, woven with the unmistakable voice of a woman.

Alarmed, I asked my buddies who had cracked open an eye, "Did you hear that?"

"Yes, they're screwing."

"Lukin is a traitor."

We all jumped out of bed like soldiers about to enter into combat. In a clearly desperate gesture, Jonás and Antonín grabbed the pillows from the bed in the event they had to repel a massive attack.

"You've betrayed the cause!" I yelled at Lukin, covering my eyes in disgust, in horror. Still I caught sight of the woman with whom he romped on the floor; it was Sonia, his ex-wife.

Realizing he'd been found out, Lukin threw Sonia aside, sprang to his feet, and said to her, "I'm sorry, but I don't need you anymore."

"I've come back, and this is my home, so I'm staying," a resolute Sonia answered.

"Fine, but you'll sleep on the couch in the living room," said Lukin, giving in, then he looked at us shamefaced and added, "I'm sorry, comrades, but I can't throw her out at this time of night. I'm not some merciless dog."

And then we knew that all was lost.

The next morning the change of seasons began—Sonia had been a clear precursor. We woke up bright and early because of the great tumult in the street and the exciting, rich scent wafting in through the windows with the morning breeze. There they were, all together, rearranging their furniture and looking for a husband. In near unison, we gave a broad collective yawn, followed by a sigh, as though awakening from the same dream. Already we could feel our spouses' trembling, the fear that accompanied the expectation of their distant yet inevitable leave-taking. One after the other we got up, hardly saying a word, as we did every year when the time came to return home and postpone once more the consolidation of our utopia. But this year, the year of the harshest winter in our history, we all left with the certainty that we had come closer than ever before.

MAROONED

Jean Rhys

They say when trouble comes close ranks, and so the white people did.
But we were not in their ranks. The Jamaican ladies had never approved
of my mother, "because she pretty like pretty self," Christophine said.

She was my father's second wife, far too young for him, they thought,
and, worse still, a Martinique girl. When I asked her why so few people
came to see us, she told me that the road from Spanish Town to Coulibri
Estate where we lived was very bad and that road repairing was now a
thing of the past. (My father, visitors, horses, feeling safe in bed—all be-
longed to the past.)

Another day I heard her talking to Mr. Luttrell, our neighbor and her
only friend. "Of course they have their own misfortunes. Still waiting for
this compensation the English promised when the Emancipation Act
was passed. Some will wait for a long time."

How could she know that Mr. Luttrell would be the first who grew
tired of waiting? One calm evening he shot his dog, swam out to sea, and
was gone for always. No agent came from England to look after his property—Nelson's Rest it was called—and strangers from Spanish Town
rode up to gossip and discuss the tragedy.

"Live at Nelson's Rest? Not for love or money. An unlucky place."

Mr. Luttrell's house was left empty, shutters banging in the wind.
Soon the black people said it was haunted, they wouldn't go near it. And
no one came near us.

I got used to a solitary life, but my mother still planned and hoped—
perhaps she had to hope every time she passed a looking glass.

She still rode about every morning not caring that the black people
stood about in groups to jeer at her, especially after her riding clothes
grew shabby (they notice clothes, they know about money).

Then one day, very early, I saw her horse lying down under the frangipani tree. I went up to him but he was not sick, he was dead and his eyes were black with flies. I ran away and did not speak of it for I thought if I told no one it might not be true. But later that day, Godfrey found him, he had been poisoned. "Now we are marooned," my mother said, "now what will become of us?"

Godfrey said, "I can't watch the horse night and day. I too old now. When the old time go, let it go. No use to grab at it. The Lord make no distinction between black and white, black and white the same for Him. Rest yourself in peace for the righteous are not forsaken." But she couldn't. She was young. How could she not try for all the things that had gone so suddenly, so without warning? "You're blind when you want to be blind," she said ferociously, "and you're deaf when you want to be deaf. The old hypocrite," she kept saying. "He knew what they were going to do." "The devil prince of this world," Godfrey said, "but this world don't last so long for mortal man."

THE IMAGINING OF IT

Jamaica Kincaid

Plunge ahead or buck up—so Mrs. Sweet's mother would say to her when she was a child, a tall thin girl all bones covered with skin, and she was afraid of the larger girls and the larger than anything boys, and would be so afraid of them that just to walk past them on the street was impossible; and earlier than that, when she was afraid of cows, for no reason at all, only that they were cows and had horns, so she was afraid of them and to walk by a pasture where these animals were fenced in and tethered to iron stakes driven into the ground was impossible for her to do: Plunge ahead, put one foot in front of the other, straighten your back and your shoulders and everything else that is likely to slump, buck up and go forward, and in this way, every obstacle, be it physical or only imagined, falls face down in obeisance and in absolute defeat, for to plunge ahead and buck up will always conquer adversity, so Mrs. Sweet's mother had said to her when she was a child, thin in body and soul, and this caused her mother much pain and great shame, for her child—the young Mrs. Sweet—needed to have drummed into her very being the clichéd words of the victorious.

And so: Plunge ahead, buck up, aim for a triumphant outcome, death being superior to failure, death is sometimes a triumph, and all this made up the amniotic fluid in which Mrs. Sweet lived when she was a child: In this way Mrs. Sweet learned to drive a car, learned to love the stark realities of her life with Mr. Sweet (he never loved her, not then, not now, she accepted it, now then and now again), took out a loan from the bank to buy the Shirley Jackson house, the house in which they lived, and it was a nice house, with views of mountains and waterfalls and meadows of flowers native to the New England landscape, and farms that cultivated food especially delicious to animals who would then be slaughtered and eaten by someone quite familiar to the slaughtered animals, friends of

Mr. and Mrs. Sweet and their children: the young Heracles and the hidden beautiful Persephone; in the far distance, Mrs. Sweet could see the beautiful Mrs. Burley—her long yellow hair in a braid cascading silently down her back and coming to rest just below her shoulder blades—a young cheese-maker milking her cows and her goats, and from this milk she would make some rare cheese and delicious yogurt that Mrs. Sweet would purchase and the rest of her family would hate: Mr. Sweet, because he hated everything about Mrs. Sweet, especially her enthusiasms, and these were: growing species of rare flowers from seeds she had gone hunting for in temperate Asia, cooking, and knitting, especially that infernal knitting. Oh Mom! Oh Mom! That would be the sound of the young Heracles. And the love and contempt and indifference that came toward Mrs. Sweet from her beloved young Heracles seemed at once to be as natural as a sweetly cool breeze that will unexpectedly change the mood of a group of people justifiably angry, or a group of people whose every need and expectation is satisfied and still they search for happiness! By that time (then, now, and then again), Mrs. Sweet had buried her past—in the cement that composes memory, even though she knew quite well that cement deteriorates, falls apart, and reveals eventually whatever it was meant to conceal.

Plunge ahead, buck up, and Mrs. Sweet did just that, as she gathered up Mr. Sweet's dropped clothes and the soiled bath towels and the sheets and the children's clothes, blouses from Wet Seal for the beautiful Persephone and trousers from somewhere else she could not pronounce, t-shirts for the young Heracles bought at a store called Manhattan, though it was located in a city far from the actual place known as Manhattan, and all the articles of clothing and dry goods that a seemingly prosperous American family might use. Mrs. Sweet washed all the clothing and other such things in the washing machine (known to her now, but unknown to her then, when she was that easily defeated child) and dried them in a clothes-drying machine and then folded the towels and other such things, and she got out the ironing board and ironed all of Mr. Sweet's shirts and trousers, too, for she loved him so, and wanted him to appear to everyone who glimpsed him for the first time as if he had just stepped out of a display in the window of a store called Love: dignified and worthy of respect. All this made her tired, in body and mind equally—the work of it, the imagining of it: clean clothing for two children and

Mr. Sweet, making them look as if they lived in a mansion on a promi-
nent street in Manhattan, or as if he lived in a village in New England
with a wife and mother who had no idea of how to be her own true self.
But to Mrs. Sweet, to whom he was actually and legally wedded, all this
was something else: Here she is plunging ahead and bucking up, too: and
walking on air, on nothing visible to the human eye, and she did not fall
into oblivion or whatever substance was made to disguise oblivion, and
she went on to the next thing and the next thing and the thing after that,
and each thing and each nothing she conquered, and she went on in her
ways, looking after her husband, tending her children, looking up at the
moon (quarter, half, or full) to see if it was in a shroud of clouds (rain
tomorrow, in any case), and feeling happy, whatever that is, Then and
Now!

WRITING IN SHIFTING SPACE

Kwame Anthony Appiah, Marlon James, Jamaica Kincaid,
Valeria Luiselli, and Colum McCann, with Eric Banks

KWAME ANTHONY APPIAH: In Tsitsi Dangarembga's novel *Nervous Conditions*, the protagonist says something like, "I've been told there's a difference between expatriates and missionaries, but I can't remember the explanation." Where I grew up, expatriates replaced the missionaries at independence. Many of them were perfectly nice people, no doubt, but they weren't committed to the place. One of the differences in the way that I've moved is that I am deeply committed to where I am now. I'm not planning to go back. I visit Ghana, but I don't think of it as my home anymore. It certainly shaped me—but I don't think of myself as an expatriate, and I don't like the word.

JAMAICA KINCAID: Expats—the way I became familiar with the word—were these sort of rancid people from England who came and sat around, and we did things for them. They were always supposedly going back to England, though they never did. They formed a community in which they were by themselves, or they were completely dependent on us. It was a group of privileged people who were incredibly lazy.

When I think of myself in America, I think of myself not as an expat. I think that would be very difficult. Even James Baldwin might have had trouble calling himself an expat. A black person is not an expat anywhere. When most people here see me, they don't think, *There's a black person from the Caribbean.* Their first reaction is, *She's black,* or *African-American.* If we were a group of people who went to Eton in England, we would be expats.

MARLON JAMES: When I was living in Jamaica, I worked in advertising. I was surrounded by expats, and my view of them was basically mediocre people from abroad who couldn't hack it in their own countries, so they'd come to the "third world," because some locals still go what I call "white crazy" in Jamaica. I actually got in arguments with some of these transplants. I'd say, "You and I both know you could never hack it on Madison Avenue. That's why you're here: because we're idiots every time you open your mouths."

I'd rather be called a refugee before I'm called an expat. I think of the laziness, and I think of the mediocrity, and I still think of people doing jobs that Jamaicans can do. I became very self-conscious when I came here on a work permit: Every year my school has to advertise my job to pretty much the whole American population, and every year the school has to convince Homeland Security or Immigration that the Jamaican is still the best person, and every year I have to prove that I'm better than hundreds of candidates who applied. So I don't feel much like an expat. That term implies an ease of being in a place that you do not have to participate in. I participate in the life of this country. I'm involved in things like Black Lives Matter. It never occurred to me that I'd have the luxury of wearing white linen suits or befriending a comandante because I would leave first when revolution happens anyway.

COLUM McCANN: The term has the tinkle of ice in the glass. It's Hong Kong and the balcony, and it just doesn't work for me. Coming from Ireland, we would never term ourselves expats. It seems to me that "to emigrate" means to wound oneself, and to leave one's country is a form of memory-making. The term "to be an emigrant," "to be an immigrant," is very important to the idea of the Irish experience. However, in more recent years, the Irish have become commuters, and we sort of belong in several different places all at once.

I'll tell you a quick story about talking to John Berger, who had been away from England (he would crucify the term "expat"). We were in Paris, and we were a tiny little bit overserved. We became intimately acquainted with a couple of darkly tinted bottles. I knew John's work inside out, and I'd been quoting it and saying all these things, and I said to him, late in the evening, "John, John, where are you from?" And he looks at me. "Well, you know, I'm from London." But then I said, "Where are you *from*-from?" And he said, "I am a patriot of elsewhere." I thought that was absolutely extraordinary, and I think it speaks to the experience of people on the panel here today.

VALERIA LUISELLI: I've been called many different things since I came to the U.S. eight years ago. Things that I never knew I *was*, or I never *knew* I was. "Alien" is a great term. First "alien nonresident," then "alien resident for tax purposes but not for immigration purposes," then "alien resident." I think now I am an "alien resident" (always an alien).

A few months after I'd arrived, some really bad magazine contacted me to write a column about dating in New York from the point of view of a woman of color. I asked a friend of mine who's African-American, "What is this 'woman of color' thing? What does it mean? I'm not a woman of color." He laughed at me, and he said, "Of course you're a woman of color." It was really shocking and really a process to assume a category that had been placed upon me. Now it's something that I carry like a badge, but at that moment, it was shocking to be coined, to *have* to belong to an invented segment of the population.

I've never been called "expat" before. It's not a term that I like. It's also very Anglo-Saxon. There isn't a term in Spanish that's quite like expat, so it isn't a term that I've ever used to define my own being and not-being. It presupposes a fatherland, the patria, and it presupposes, also, a very strong bond with the center that one has exited from; I don't have that relationship with any country. I've never lived in any country for more than a few years.

ERIC BANKS: You once said, "I decided New York was the place I wanted to live because it was the place where I felt exactly the right equilibrium between being foreign and being at home," which I think is wonderfully put.

LUISELLI: So many people here are somehow foreign to the city and always in the process of coming to terms with it, or becoming involved with it in different ways. Something that I've always struggled with is being a Mexican in New York. There's a big Mexican population here, and most of this population is invisible. In a physical sense, most Mexicans in New York work underground, either in the kitchens or the bodegas or in the delis that we walk through. My daughter once asked me, "Who's down there?"

when we were walking on the metal flaps in the sidewalk. She used to think it was a scary space, that there might be witches or something. I said, "No, it's a lot of Mexicans," so she really loves peeking in now and saying, "¡Hola!" But it's an invisible population that's rarely mapped. To find my own space within that Mexican population has been a challenge. Finding a sense of belonging and distance at the same time is something that I work on every day.

BANKS: Colum, is this an experience that you would identify with?

McCANN: I don't feel foreign here at all, and a lot of the people that I know, especially writers, don't feel foreign here at all. One of the things that I think is brave and tough and muscular about the American literary establishment is you are allowed to come here and to retain your foreignness. If you're Sasha Hemon, you can still be Bosnian and American at the same time. There are so many writers—Junot Díaz, myself, Yiyun Li—who are allowed to come here, and they don't strip away the citizenship of where you came from. That's a very brave, American idea, and it wouldn't necessarily happen in other parts of the world. It would be very difficult to go to Ireland and to be a person of two countries, so we should applaud some of the democratic and radical experience that goes on here, that sort of radical welcoming where you can come here and be someone new directly on the next day. I applaud that notion, that I'm allowed to hold on to my country, because I couldn't come here if I had to say good-bye to my country. I couldn't come here if I had to be labeled an expat. That would just wound me too deeply.

KINCAID: I certainly would like to ask Junot Díaz about that—but mainly, you really ought to think about what you say, because I think it's very easy for you. You're a white man. You have a huge, distinguished history of coming from Ireland. There are a lot of Irish people who came to America and disenfranchised a lot of other people in the process of becoming "white." It sounds wonderful, and it's a nice thing for you to say about America. Americans would really like that, a lot of them, but in contrast to you, I didn't feel I was just stepping into this grand literature and welcomed. I still don't feel like that at all, so I would not universalize that so much. Just say, "I, a white guy from Ireland, had this experience." I'm really glad that you had it. I don't wish to be a white guy, but I'm glad that white guys enjoy themselves so much.

JAMES: There's a difference between New York or California and America. For example, my second novel was published by Riverhead, but everybody else rejected it. My first one was rejected by eighty people. It's one of the reasons why a bunch of writers of color have declared that we will never be on a panel on diversity ever again. You've heard me say it publicly. Because I think there is this lip service diversity: I'm allowed to be Jamaican, but a certain kind of Jamaican, a certain kind of antiseptic Jamaican. I agree with Kincaid on this.

There's a problem when a Nigerian writer goes, "There is my Nigerian voice, and there is my Nigerian-for-America voice." I'm not talking about right-wing people; I'm talking about people who speak about diversity and the neoliberal and so on. I think we are allowed to hold on to our identity, but to me even the "allowed" part may be problematic. I'm not asking for permission.

APPIAH: I came here in my late twenties, and two things do strike me as welcoming about this country. One is that though I came here a long time ago and I still talk like this, when I say I'm an American, people don't fall about laughing. Whereas I think in many other countries you could go to, if you didn't talk like the regular people, they would. Here, I think, citizenship, which I have, is kind of it. We have a long history of exclusion, but citizenship is open now, in principle, to anybody who can get in. It can be hard to get in. It's easier to get in if you have a PhD in philosophy from Cambridge, but once you're in, you're in. I like that.

Before I got here, I had read James Baldwin and Richard Wright. I knew about Martin Luther King. I knew America was a racist country where you risked being shot. I knew all the basic facts, but I had no real sense of the African-American experience, meaning the experience of the descendants of America's slaves, and yet every black family in this country that I met welcomed me in as if I was a brother, even though I talked weird and I didn't really have any connection with them. Now I do; I've been a professor of African-American studies. But I didn't grow up with it. Sometimes when I think about that, I'm moved almost to tears by the welcome that I experienced, by people like Skip's family, whom I got to know when I first got here. They didn't know anything about my life, and I didn't know anything about theirs, but they let me in immediately in a kind of mad way, and it was very moving to me. So I do feel I've been welcomed in a bunch of ways that I don't think would happen in a lot of other places.

In a way, we got a bit stuck with the "expatriate" word. The thought behind this was how the experience of moving around affects your relationship to things like language. I grew up speaking two languages, and one of them was English. I grew up, as many people in the world did, listening to American television as a child. The sound of American voices—black voices, white voices, Southern voices, Northern voices—was in my ear long before I got here. It wasn't my language, but it didn't seem strange to me when I got here. An awful lot of people in the world live in countries where English is the government language, and in those countries, *Dallas* was playing in the '70s, and you got to hear it. So America didn't seem so strange in that sense. And as I said, we were brought up in a house, a Pan-Africanist household, to read Baldwin and Wright. Actually, Wright talks about part of my family in one of his books, so we knew some of these people. I feel that it's not like the Anglophone expatriate experience where you come from England to this strange place, and everybody talks in a language you don't know except when they're talking to you and so on. It's not like that at all. It's a very different kind of move in relation to language.

LUISELLI: To add something to the theme of welcome and not welcome that we sort of left hanging: I also don't feel quite welcome as a Mexican here when there are stadiums full of people shouting, "Let's build a wall!" There are many levels of belonging, and in many of those levels of belonging, I don't feel welcome, either. But I do think that the literary world here is larger than the one in Mexico and more diverse—more international, but also more diverse racially. Most Mexican writers are white, and there's very little recognition of writers who don't write in Spanish in Mexico.

I learned English when I was five years old while living in South Korea in an American military school. The community was founded by soldiers who had decided to live in Korea and had Korean-American kids there. Because my parents were fiercely nationalist as Mexicans, they wouldn't allow me to watch TV, because the American base only played

American TV. When I arrived here, I spoke weird English—I also spent time as a child in South Africa, so my English was more South African, and I had no knowledge of American idiomatic expressions. That has been a really difficult thing, to relearn English, although it's the language I learned to write and read in before Spanish.

KINCAID: Well, I didn't see television until I was nineteen years of age. I'm older than everybody here, I think, so I don't have the familiarity that you talk about as formative. I grew up in what was—well, Britain wasn't a colonial power anymore, but we didn't know that. No one told us. So I don't have an ease with American culture, though I did always want to look like an African-American woman in *Ebony* magazine. I loved *Ebony* magazine, and I loved African-American culture in the way I saw it through that lens. But the thing you're talking about, familiarity with American culture giving you ease, I still don't have it.

In relation to language, I am still very much a person of colonial Britain. My relationship to literature begins with Chaucer. My writing is not at all informed by American culture, and I do see the problem my works present to an American, who might always be wondering why the sentences are so long, why the repetition. My influences are the *Oxford English Dictionary*, the King James version of the Bible, Milton, and no one understands why that would be. When I sit down to write, I sit down to think about the world, it has nothing to do with American anything. The American love of a story that has a beginning and an end, and the absolutely hateful thing called *closure*: I have no interest in it at all.

That's very productive for me, but I think unsatisfying to an American readership. We are on a powerful continent, and this powerful continent produces so much disturbance that the citizens of the continent would like, when they sit down to read a book, for that book to offer some solace about the human condition. I insist on offering none.

BANKS: That raises the interesting question of audience. How much is this something you think about, Marlon?

JAMES: I didn't realize this until somebody pointed it out to me, but the American section of my book reads totally differently than the Jamaican section. It's not just that the subject matter changed; she said she could tell

I had changed. That complements something Colum said. I know I could never write that novel in Jamaica. I think there is a sort of a freedom to be exactly the type of writer that's in my head, and to have everything that is up here come down exactly that way on the page (I don't mean without editing). Being uprooted can actually become a safe space where I can create. Especially when I'm writing very political stuff, like *A Brief History of Seven Killings*. Being in my home country would have resulted in a different kind of novel. I actually think it would have resulted in a failure of nerve. I'm only talking about myself—there are lots of people who are perfectly capable of writing really explosive stuff in their home countries; look at the great South African literature that came out during apartheid. But I think I needed that kind of suspended space.

BANKS: When you talk about that "suspended space," is it something very specific about the place you ended up, or is it more the experience of being somewhere else?

JAMES: I think it's the experience of being somewhere else. I've written the bulk of two novels on the road. I wrote my second novel when I was on tour for the first one. I just got used to writing in shifting space.

I have a desk. I have an office. I have never been there. Even when I'm home, I have an office, I have a computer, I have everything, and I'll crouch down on the floor in the living room and write, or go downstairs or something. I don't know at what point it happened, but instead of waiting for this state of flux to be over so I could create, I decided to create in flux.

McCANN: I'd agree with Marlon. I was just struck with this image, for whatever reason... Truck drivers, to keep themselves awake, have two tricks: They cut their fingers, sort of wound themselves, to keep themselves awake as they're driving down the road—and they also inhale sulfur. They light matches, and then they flick them out, and they inhale the sulfur.

JAMES: How do you know these things?

McCANN: I was on the road for a long time. When I came to the States, I took a bicycle across the country for a year and a half. I ended up doing about eight thousand miles on the road, and I met all sorts of crazy people. It seems to me that writers who come to this place do the same kind of thing. We're looking for that moment of struck-ness. We're looking for that moment of pain, in order to remember or to keep ourselves awake.

LUISELLI: The matches trick always does it for me.

McCANN: Sulfur jags your brain. It gets your brain to go *whoosh*.

LUISELLI: Absolutely. Immediately.

McCANN: Immigration is a form of sulfurizing.

BANKS: Valeria, *The Story of My Teeth* was a collaboration from a distance: You were working with people in Mexico City in the creation of the novel. Can you say something about that?

LUISELLI: I was trying to write my second novel, and I was trying to write it in English. I've been writing in both languages for a long time, but my three published books were originally written in Spanish. I was commissioned by a big art gallery called the Jumex Collection. It's one of the most important contemporary art collections in the world, but their money comes from a juice factory that holds a monopoly. It's called Jumex (jugos mexicanos) and their revenues buy contemporary art. I thought that relationship was disquieting, so when they commissioned me to write a fictional piece for the gallery, I said I would be more interested to write for the factory. They said no, so I said I wouldn't do it. We negotiated a bit, and finally we found a way to make it possible. I sent an installment, printed like a chapbook, to the factory, and they handed it over to different workers to see who might be interested in reading it.

Twelve people were interested. They formed a reading group and got together once a week to read the installments, and they criticized it and suggested changes, or just tried to interpret it. That helped me a lot, because I never know what I'm doing when I'm writing. I would listen to those sessions and then write the next installment—with no previous plan, of course, because I had to hear what the workers said first. It's very nineteenth-century, actually.

BANKS: It's a serial novel.

LUISELLI: It's a Dickensian kind of thing, just with email.

It brought me back to Spanish as well. Real Spanish, the Spanish of a group of workers in discussion. During that period, I called my uncle a lot (the main character is partly based on him). My uncle was a salesman in a big market. He's a big storyteller; he always tells stories about the things that he sells, so I heard his voice. It was a way of connecting back to real Spanish, not extraterritorial Spanish, which is what I mostly hear and speak now.

McCANN: I love that idea of real Spanish and accessing the old language. I've written a book about the homeless people who live in the subway tunnels of New York; a book about a gay Muslim ballet dancer, Rudolf Nureyev; a book about Romani people in Slovakia; and a book called *Let the Great World Spin,* which takes place in New York. The whole time, over the course of nine books, I always think that I'm still writing an Irish novel, and that's really important to me. Even if this accent gets in under my accent, as far as I'm concerned, I'm still always writing about the place that I came from. Is that old-fashioned? Is that silly? I don't know, but I cling to the notion that no matter what, I'm still writing an Irish novel.

AUDIENCE: How do you know when you belong, if you live in many places and you keep traveling?

McCANN: Michael Ondaatje, one of my favorite writers, talks about the international mongrels of the world. He's born in Sri Lanka, educated in England, goes to Canada, and writes his first book about a turn-of-the-century jazz musician down in New Orleans. I think he belongs in that sort of *elsewhere*. But that, for a writer, brings up several issues of cultural arrogance, economic arrogance, gender arrogance, and so on. You know: What do you have a right to talk about?

JAMES: I think *belonging* is a really expansive and really reductive thing at the same time. I feel I belong wherever I flip open my laptop and start writing, in a way. That's important to me. Going back to Jamaica, I realized how much home was important to me, and also how little I belong there. A certain lack of belonging is important for a writer.

LUISELLI: I don't know if you have kids or not, Marlon, but I think that when you do have kids, that sense of belonging begins in PTA meetings, and it's horrible to belong.

KINCAID: Yeah, but that's a different thing. A parent is a parent, and a writer is a writer.

LUISELLI: But we are both things, come on.

KINCAID: No, I take exception to the PTA as belonging. I think the PTA is belonging to the parent, but a writer is not—

LUISELLI: I just cannot disassociate myself as parent and writer.

KINCAID: I haven't read your writing, so I can't say that makes you not a good writer.

LUISELLI: Well, maybe tonight you will.

KINCAID: That's just not acceptable. A writer is a writer, and a parent is—

LUISELLI: I don't agree.

McCANN: I would love to say that I can be a writer and a parent both at the same time. Sometimes I become the son of my son, for instance, in that I am fascinated by what he is fascinated by, and he leads me in all sorts of different directions. I think you can embrace both at once. You can helix these things together.

AUDIENCE: Do you think about writing intentionally or strategically as people of color or people who are not from the "first world"? Marlon, you were talking about just writing for yourself in your head—but you also know that white people are listening, Americans are listening. How do you play with that?

JAMES: There's a danger if you think about that too much. The novel, the poem, or even the painting that is in your head is the one that should come down on the page. Otherwise you start to write by committee (and the committee hasn't even formed yet!) or you start to second-guess your audience. Is there a price to pay for that? Yeah. It's been a long road for writers like me to get published, but I have to trust that the writing will find its audience, whether it takes five years or ten years.

There are certain things I don't do. I don't pander to an audience. I don't drop the Jamaican part off. Somebody once said to me, "I couldn't make it through your book." I said, "I don't give refunds," because I'm at the point where I don't care. I teach creative writing, and one of the hardest things to get students to stop doing is pre-compromising. Nobody's told you you're difficult yet, and you're already pre-compromising with your story? I had to un-teach myself that, because I came out of advertising, and advertising is all about compromise. Audience is a matter of craft, not art. Is this as clear as it could have been? Is this a place for a colon or a semicolon or a comma? That's what I think about audience.

AUDIENCE: Do you intentionally play with structure or form when you're writing about place?

JAMES: I try to reflect a place but also subvert it, twist it, even violate it. Some of the stuff I've written is based on true events, but I didn't write nonfiction because I wanted to reserve the novelist's right to invent.

KINCAID: When I'm writing, I am only true to the thing I'm writing. I find the contemporary obsession with the consideration of others in writing really disturbing, and I almost can't respect a readership that would expect me to please them.

AUDIENCE: I would like to know what you make of the notion of selective or elective affinities. Because nobody here came here by force.

JAMES: I don't know to what I extent I made a choice to come here. I came here because I ran out of choices. I came here because as a writer in a territory where writers wouldn't go very far, as a gay man in a country that's not very keen on that stuff, part of it was running out of options.

Baldwin chose to go to France, but he also had to. He *had* to. I'm not going to make conclusions for everybody here, but I think it's more than a caprice. There is an urgency when we leave where we are. That's why the term "expat" is kind of tricky, if not outright bad. Last night, I was talking about how terrible the word "immigrant" is. Certain people get to be "immigrants," and some people get to be "migrants," and some people get to be "expats," and some people get to be "refugees." But yeah, for me at least, there was some choice. I could afford my plane ticket. But there was a sense of running out of options and a sense of needing to leave. Not necessarily fleeing, but certainly leaving as an act of saving oneself.

McCANN: My affinity would be to story and to storytelling and the ability to nuance the debate, and to complicate the notions of place by bringing in new stories and sort of mashing them all together. The place that I belong is in the process of stories and storytelling.

LUISELLI: I began my life as a reader perhaps a little bit late, when I was fifteen or sixteen. I was in high school in India, and I had a very good literature teacher who read to us and gave us Langston Hughes and Nella Larsen, and I began reading about Harlem and the Harlem Renaissance in that context. I had grown up in South Africa, but I couldn't live there beyond when I was fifteen because my parents left. The place I knew I had to eventually get to was Harlem, and I've been living in Harlem since I came here. I guess it is through story that you sort of fall in love with a place. There's a beautiful line by Langston Hughes, who says that he was already in love with Harlem before he arrived there, and I think that I was already in love with Harlem when I arrived, because of him and other people. So yeah, that constellation of writers—there was also a group of Mexican writers living in Harlem during the Renaissance, most of them unknown, widely unread, that I eventually started reading. They became part of the cohort of ghosts that made me feel at home.

This transcript is adapted from a conversation at the 2016 PEN World Voices Festival.

KYLE & JASON

Marlon James

This is a story about Kyle and Jason. "Kyle" and "Jason" are names that rich boys get. Uptown Kingston boys. Jamaican boys with skin lighter than Daddy's fat wallet. They live in places with names like "Norbrook." At high school recess, they close ranks with other rich boys, uptown boys. But Kyle and Jason are good boys. Well, Jason is. Jason lent me all his Smiths records. Kyle stole my Phil Collins and said, "Faggot, I'd never borrow that shit from you," when I asked for it back. We were all boys in an all-boys high school, puberty bursting out of school uniforms, drunk on dumb youth.

Kyle and Jason aren't actually called "Kyle" and "Jason." I made those names up, because both men are still roaming. Right now, Jason roams New York City, and may very well be here tonight. Right now, Kyle is standing at the end of a Burger King drive-through in Kingston, trying to remember which person he forgot.

"Bredren, let off a hundred dollars, now? Fifty? Twenty? Ten? Where do I know you from?"

"You still have my Phil Collins record."

"What?"

"Never mind. No, you don't know me."

Jason walks New York because Jamaica is a place he punched a hole through. He can never go back. Kyle walks Kingston looking for the next woman, looking for the next man to save.

Let's do this in reverse.

2016

I haven't seen either of them in over ten years, maybe fifteen, but I hear:

"You know about Jason, right? He had to leave after he got out of prison, but there was no place for him here. Not after what happened to him."

"'*To* him'? Don't you mean 'after what he did'?"

We have to forgive the unforgivable. "He didn't do anything to me. I hear he's back on it, cocaine this time."

"Oh. Well, cocaine is cool. Maybe that's how he deals with the years he was on crack. I mean, everybody in Fleetwood Mac used to hit coke. As long as it's not crack again."

2016

Kyle is still on the street. Now he's forty-seven, which means he's been a crack addict for thirty years. Lean and ripped, but crackhead-ripped, which means each muscle is punctuated with a bruise from sleeping on the sidewalk, or from a man who finally thought of his wife after getting his dick sucked by a dude.

"At least they're not fucking me." Mm-hm.

But no crackhead goes downtown unless he plans to get fucked, 'cause that pays double. But he gets half, because there are boys here one-third his age. His friend the musician came down to see his son, then vanished for a month. Turns out he went to the crackhouse in Ravinia. That weekend, he OD'ed, and his body sat there rotting for weeks, while people tripped all around him.

Kyle doesn't do crackhouses. He brushes his teeth, looks for wounded women on a mission. He's living with one now. She will save him, until he falls—then he'll blame her, and she'll try harder, and he will fall again, and blame her, and she will try harder, and he will fall again, and blame her, and she'll try harder, and he'll fall again, and blame her. And she will try harder, and harder, and harder, until she learns—maybe in six months, maybe in a year, maybe two—that she was only looking for a mission; he was just looking to live rent-free.

2006

Jason is out of prison, and I see him in a nightclub.

"Did you see Jason?"

"Yeah, I did."

"Did he recognize you?"

"We were never that close."

"Well, there is one person who will never take drugs again."

"Why not?"

"I don't know, after what he did?"

"But there's nothing left now. What do people with nothing do?"

"I don't know, he's coming over. Dance with me."

2006

"Did you hear about Kyle?"

"What, he's on to heroin? That fucker could never afford heroin."

"His family disappeared."

"What?"

"Yeah, just like that. His family just vanished, poof. They got tired of him breaking them, so they just left. House is as they left it. They just left the country and didn't tell anybody they were going. Not friends, not family, no one. They couldn't risk Kyle following them."

"How the fuck would Kyle follow them? The only reason he hasn't overdosed is that he can't afford that much drugs."

"He'd find a way. Anyway, they're all gone."

1996

Kyle is at KFC hoping some guy he vaguely remembers will buy him a two-piece chicken dinner. He knows everybody who's still on drugs, but he's not. Crack is for losers. Crack is for the '80s, and this is 1996. At least he's not Jason.

Jason. The last Monday night in September, they find Jason naked on his lawn. Men are always naked when you find them. He was at his parents'; they took him out of detox because they were a respectable family. Detox made him paranoid. The family was plotting a birthday party. Jason thought they were plotting. When they found him, he was still clutching the hammer. He had bludgeoned his girlfriend's head off and had started working on his mother.

1986

Crack is a ghetto disease in America. In Jamaica, it means you're young, and it's so fucking messy dealing with coke. In Kyle's house, there is crack on the counter like spilled sugar cubes. All the cool kids are doing it. Sounds like a cliché even then, but all the cool kids are doing it. Cool guys, cute guys, guys who trip and fall and land between girls' legs.

Why do people take drugs? Life's too hard?

Crack wasn't cheap. Nobody with a hard life could afford drugs.

Why do people take drugs?

Why do they *keep* taking drugs is easier to answer, because there's nothing to do with a life off drugs but to get back on it. Nobody wants to take the mask off 2016 to realize you're still living in an interrupted 1986.

Why do people take drugs?

Why did that woman cheat on her husband in the movie *Unfaithful?* Because the fucking drugs are there, and so are we. Because the drugs are here.

This essay is adapted from a talk at the 2016 PEN World Voices Festival.

DAY PASSES

Anne Enright

So I am in a small town in Honduras having my cigarette, because if there is one thing I love when I am away from my children it is killing myself with Marlboro Lights. Though there are quicker ways to get killed here in Honduras, where I am writing a piece about land tenure for an Irish aid agency. There is the big fat gun of the guy protecting the little restaurant, and there are the many other guns, the private militias the narcos the army the customs and excise the cops the gangs of course the lawyers the journalists and other private citizens who feel a bit vulnerable, given the circumstances—not so many among the poor campesinos whose land is being taken away from them, but still—lots and lots of guns here in Honduras. Apart from the aid workers, of course. The aid workers have no guns. Now I love aid workers and I sort of resent aid workers because they are better than me, morally, and they also have better stories and there is nothing I could write—I am a fiction writer—to match one of their littlest stories. So this aid worker Sally points into the little town square and says "that is where they left her head."

OK. The narcos launder their money through the local market women, they give them money and then take charge of their little bank accounts, many small bills, many women, fifty or a hundred dollars at a time. These women with their onions, or rice, or piles of bad T-shirts, and one of these women, her husband is a drunk and he takes the fifty bucks to go drinking so she can't put it in the bank for the narcos and the narcos come and they dismember her and leave her body parts scattered around the town and in the town square and nailed to the local lamp posts. "Over there," she says. Thanks for that, Sally. So I put out my cigarette because I really need a beer now and I thank God or biology I have no interest in cocaine, which is the dirtiest thing in the world, after oil. I have no interest in cocaine because when I tried it, long ago, I was that boring, that bored, on cocaine, yakety yak. I ended up talking about the price of my own sunglasses. Yakety yak.

I mean I am a really interesting drunk. I am a deeply interesting and sometimes tortured human being—I don't mean tortured the way the narcos do torture I mean the way Sylvia Plath did torture. "My Body Is a Cage" is my favorite song title by Arcade Fire. My Body Is a Cage—the problem is getting out of there without letting the door slam behind you, because the greatest escape of all, unfortunately and of course, is death. Meanwhile, there are day passes—sex, meditation, psychosis, dissociative states, the endorphin rush of exercise, the top of the mountain and the freewheel cycle downhill: Let us not forget poetry, the touch of someone you love; there is, when you think about it, love itself. But so effortful all of them, so exhausting, this battle through the ego to escape the ego, this pushing of the body to be free of the body, when all you really have to do to escape your sad sack of bones and flesh is—whatever. Take a pill.

Or go for a swim, perhaps. I am mildly addicted to the sea. I like the way the salt water holds you up, and slaps you about a bit. The sea is plentiful and cheap. No one gets hurt when you swim in the sea. You are, as you float on it, connected to every other beach in the round world. There, in front of you, chopped about by the advancing waves, is the horizon line and this does some secret, muscular thing to your gaze. After five minutes swimming toward it, your brain will open: simple as a window in April.

You know the smell of a baby is addictive to its mother? The smell of her baby lights up the addiction centers of the brain in that poor, wrecked, non-smoking, non-drinking woman who is drunk on the smell of her new baby, dizzy, incoherent with it all. It doesn't work for everyone, of course. But yes, I inhaled.

And can you imagine. Can you just imagine what is happening in that new brain. How mad that baby is for its mother? What chaos and perfection is there, and what do you do, when that is gone? You know all the drugs I ever took—and there weren't that many—but I get it, I think I do get it. The aim is not to bring love back—that impossibility—the aim is to turn the absence of love into bliss. Absence into bliss. Bliss into boredom. The aim is to disconnect.

You are fifteen years old, you are sixteen years old. And all you want to do is leave. You are nobody's baby, not anymore. And all you want to do is leave. How cool is that? It is very cool. To be so in control of it all. To be nowhere. And in control of nowhere. To wear your wonderful sunglasses late into the night.

This essay is adapted from a talk at the 2016 PEN World Voices Festival.

WHITE PEOPLE EATING WHITE FOOD

francine j. harris

You have not gone up against the plaster wall
with real plastic forks, lately, or ruined much dental

work with the metal studs hanging too fat and too quick
from your bleached Hanes, or let the overturn of your cock

puss. You lay in white sheets eating boxed potatoes
from a sectioned paper plate, watching reality's

skinny Texan as he speed eats gummy worms, and slinkys
on commercial break, in a frame ad, then back to themed water

parks, with slip tubulature, like jellied condoms, like sweet
shower liners, such that the gaunt contestant stuffs

rough napkins inside his cheeks to keep. This is that kind
of room. It sounds like pink air conditioning. Such as the sort

is worn out. Who has white fun anymore. Pink
fiberglass, insufflation. When girls ring

the downward door, you venge binge on their teeth, sucking

and hollering *fuck, come.* You complain of night terrors.
It's such faint panic. Such wicker basket frantic while the sound

of Amazon's stick gets lost in the powdery mattress pads
like a Utah runway buffering white planes. You have large

salt bags bloating. a pillow between your legs, and a plated
grin. which burrows with its white mint, digs. eyes like peeled

white carrot. In each window, white mayfly, dead
infest, stuck to the top of your lip until you spit.

SIREN, AGAIN

Gala Mukomolova

*Let me show you what I'm all about how I make a Sprite can disappear
in my mouth*, Lil' Kim has me

thinking about poverty, mine I mean, swallowing improbable shit just
to get you off.

I'm getting texts from this poet, she wants to bend me over, fuck me til
she comes. How does it feel? Fuck me like that? *A warrior coming home,*

a young king. Ok, Odysseus, *keep it real and live good*—I guess.

Once I opened my brother's closet and found only designer sweaters: Gucci,
Armani, Versace. My slippers had cockroach goo on them. We lived four

to a one bedroom apt. He slept on the living room floor. I'd walk by him
and the neighbor girl fucking, turn on Saturday morning cartoons.

She'd blanket his ass, as if for my sake. There are so many ways to learn
the luxury of a door.

Bet it all, Playa, fuck the price. I think Lil' Kim's talking about a dice game.
I'm circling my heart but I hate being obvious.

What this poet calls *slippery*, what I call smart. Like it matters, like I'm not
pulling rent money out of a dog's ass.

I was wrong. I want everything. I want to be fucked like the wife who waited
for her soldier's return, fucked: the island, the sand, the nymph,

the lust that strands him. Fucked: the witch's sword against his dick before she opens. *Ill deep throat, I'm sayin'*

it's April, 72 degrees, I'm in love and wearing platforms. This song is just like my first years in America, *the jump off.* What I mean is reckless, performing

a kind of hope.

LAST NIGHT, I WAS TRAPPED IN THE WRONG BODY AGAIN

Tommye Blount

A downy woodpecker shakes its head the way say a scruffy-faced
teenager might. It's pulsing—the red streak running down
the middle of its crown. Or at least I think it's red in the glow
of the bird-spiked Meijer sign. Then again, this late, I'm not sure
if it's a bird at all. It could, in fact, be a teenager. A deaf 15-year-old boy—
or he'll eventually go deaf if he doesn't turn down his earphones.
I could be anyone walking toward him.

                                                   Not listening to anyone,
his ears are full of wax—but even that isn't right. No one listens
to records anymore, you see. Yet his head is full of a violent song
in the same way mine could. He's dabbing at
his phone's screen like a reflection one of the Walled Lake townies might see
before they've gone too far.

                                          In the winter months,
during the day, they walk on the lake
in a somnambulist's lurch. Not listening to the ice,
they pitch their huts and bore their holes in the floor. And there are fish
swishing in sequined gowns—their denticulate jaws mouthing
like background singers. All those scales
mimicking knives—a soundtrack to kill by.

                                        Last night, I was trapped
in the wrong body again. I fell asleep after jacking off to a freeze frame
of Christian Bale in *American Psycho*. Then I dreamed I was Christian Bale
and couldn't stop touching myself. No, I was The Dark Knight,
only Christian Bale as The Dark Knight throwing a tantrum
on set. My cowl couldn't keep up with my pout. Then I howled myself

into myself again—big and black and terrifying. I was a monster
knocking down all of the lights. I punched someone's lights out.
                        When I came to, the woodpecker
was in my hands feeding on nothing because it was dead. Or rather, the dyed teenager
who looks like a downy woodpecker is small enough to fit in my hands.
There is no music to kill. There is nothing left to hear. The red streak is no streak
but a wound. I swear, I found him, I fished the blade out.

I WANT SO DESPERATELY
TO BE FINISHED WITH DESIRE

sam sax

after all my labor
            pleasure arrives
inelegant as ever
                secondhand chandelier
onion sound
        the gutter that grunts
back at you when you spit
                    in its mouth

//

even with my hand inside him
            he's somewhere else

//

the shipwreck leaves
            the paired animal bodies
floating   & bloated with salt

//

everyone drags all their past
            lovers into bed
all their past beds
            & public toilets   & foil pipes

& park benches   & cutlasses
        & cigarettes
& the deadbolt   & the dead

//

my hand's inside him
            & he's with someone else
gone men breathing
        gone   breath on his neck

//

the brain is a maniac organ
it puppets me

//

i follow a man off the subway
            into queens   & look up
to see my life has passed

//

every text message i send
        is a tongue   pushing through the body
of the phone until it laps
            at a strained pair of eyes

//

my man wakes up next to me
            & recoils
at my hardness
        gathered at his thigh

//

two primates
      reach between each others legs
& get to work   one throws his head
      back to stare down god
while the other wants
      to leave

//

i press my naked shape
      against aquarium glass
& let the squid swarm
      my deformed organ
they're amazed how it fans out
      like a sibling
brethren & recognition

//

      every old wound dressed
in drag & daggers

//

      child of the invert & sodomite
    of the lecher in her leper print
gown of the leper bell
      & its leper sound

//

my thirst is basic
      easily quenched
water will do

//

i used to be wild
                        unripe fruit
i'd lash myself
            to any new mast
while some man stared
                        down strange
as i strained
            & galloped terribly
against his sound

PRONUNCIATION: PART ONE

Aziza Barnes

he tells me in mississippi the only laws broken concern meth and obesity.
i'm at the dude ranch listening to a black man from Oxford rap *a genocide
is a genocide* his 40 acre ballad. land & we want to put our feet in the dirt
alive. this blond soror wobbles into me *hey* & the drawl hits the rim of her
Coors Light *so you're not bi?* her lips are 2 sheets of bible paper *you're nervous? it's cause I'm from Mississippi, right?* i ask her if she has a name i can
call her. it's Nancy & she tells me i'm going to have a hard time down
here. her shirt is a scarf that falls off every time she shouts *woohoo! she
could've been anywhere tonight* the other queer black woman says to me *a
Keith Urban concert, anywhere.* my lipstick looks like shoeshine polish on
her chin & around us are approximately 7 shrines to white Jesus. *they're
mostly ironic* says the mississippians.

in my bed & alone a black thing falls out a crack in my white ceiling. a
cockroach that can fly! let's all get in bed with the queer black yankee
fuck! her androgynous sex her minstrel shuck shuck all down my chin
don't cancel my order ship that bitch back to me live! it got to the point
where chattel was less fuckable. consent is the mule we never got. a roach
wakes me up by crawling on my arm & a black man in queens new york
tells me he's envious *at least he gets to touch you.*

let's lay hands on her said the lord.
let's lay hands on her said the soror.
let's lay hands on her said the black man.
let's lay hands on her said the roaches that could fly.

TOLSTOY CAN'T SUE

Boris Akunin and Walter Mosley, with Keith Gessen

KEITH GESSEN: Having lived almost an entire life not being a novelist, why did you decide to become one?

BORIS AKUNIN: For me it was a midlife crisis. I was exactly forty, and I suddenly was afraid of the idea that my life would go on like this until I was eighty, and it would be just the same, the same, the same. I wanted to change things, and I wanted to be free. I wanted to be free financially too, and I didn't want to work with anybody anymore. I wanted to work just by myself and for myself.

WALTER MOSLEY: I was thirty-eight, and working as a computer programmer. I liked doing it. It's just that my whole life would have been the same day over and over again. It was an okay day, but not enough for a whole lifetime. I was always thinking one day I wanted to do something artistic. I was working at Mobil Oil one Saturday. I was a consultant, and I wrote a sentence: "On hot, sticky days in southern Louisiana, the fire ants swarmed." I thought, *Oh, that's good, that sounds like a book, and it's fiction, because I've never been to Louisiana. I don't know what a fire ant looks like.* I said to myself, *I'm going to write novels.* I didn't go so far as to think I was going to make money out of it. I thought I was going to write and work. At least I would feel happy writing.

GESSEN: Was there a particular kind of book that you wanted to create? How did your life as a reader feed your decision to become a writer?

AKUNIN: Being a literary translator is a great profession, but after some years, you start to get irritated by writers you translate because you get more and more experience, and you think, *Oh, come on, it's not done like this. Oh, come on, you should stop here. Who needs this landscape description here?* After a while, I thought I would try to do it myself.

MOSLEY: Reading your books, it seems to me you are trying to bring about a feeling, not of nostalgia, but of a possibility or potential inside Russia. It reminds me of writers like Jules Verne, looking back and saying, "This is an experience that you could have had." In reading what's happening in the past, you can have hope for a future.

I live in Los Angeles, and nobody reads history books. I knew there was a vibrant black population that had migrated to L.A. from the Deep South after 1945, but nobody wrote about it. It seemed to me that if I wrote about black people, specifically black male heroes, my detectives and their friends, then I would actually speak to the world. I'd speak to a bunch of black people who would say, "Hey, right, we were part of this. I remember that." And then I would speak to the rest of the country, saying, "You know, it's not just you guys. It's all these other people, all this other possibility."

GESSEN: Why did you choose noir as the vehicle for that?

MOSLEY: I wrote a book called *Gone Fishin'*. It was about two characters, Easy Rawlins and Raymond "Mouse" Alexander coming of age in the Deep South. I gave it to a whole bunch of agents and publishers, and they all said the same thing: "White people don't read about black people, black women don't like black men, and black men don't read. So who's going to buy your book?" Then I said, "Okay, I'll write a mystery." So I wrote a mystery, and they said, "Wow! A black detective! That's a really new idea." One guy said to me, "But you know there's already a black detective," and I said, "Well, you know, there's a whole bunch of white detectives." I ended up in the genre. I like it. I read other books, too, but the genre helps other people outside of the experience to come into it. Which is a great thing about the genre: All kinds of people read it.

GESSEN: What about you, Boris?

AKUNIN: Why historical fiction? Well, it gives you freedom to fantasize.

All the witnesses are dead. Nobody except some historian is going to write, "You are mistaken here." And who reads historians?

GESSEN: It's pretty tough out here for historians.

AKUNIN: Another thing is that, because I was a literature translator for such a long time, I do not have a literary style of my own. I can easily imitate any literary style, but I cannot write just like myself. When you take the nineteenth century, with a lot of great names in Russian literature, it's so easy. It's fun, because on this page you are Tolstoy, and on another page you are Dostoevsky, and there you are Chekhov. It gives your text sophistication, and you have fun. Readers are flattered: There is another sort of detective game, apart from who killed whom, because a reader tries to figure out allusions, motives, recognize characters from classical literature. It's also very easy to fool your reader because you describe a character they recognize from Tolstoy, and he's a very good guy, and in your case, he's probably, you know, a murderer in the end.

MOSLEY: And Tolstoy can't sue you.

GESSEN: In the late '90s, were you trying to give something to Russian readers who had just experienced the trauma of the end of communism?

AKUNIN: No, I just wanted to entertain them. Now that I'm older and I've become more of a bore, I feel like preaching and teaching; then I just wanted to have fun. But I understood very well, because I was in the book industry, that there was serious potential: In Russian literature, we did not have a hero, a character whom boys would like to imitate and girls would like to fall in love with, because the characters from Russian literature all love to suffer. They are very good at failing. They never win. They are never victorious. There are no Supermen. I wanted to create a Russian hero—like Walter, actually.

MOSLEY: I love Russian literature. My family on my mother's side is Russian. My favorite character is Chichikov.

AKUNIN: Chichikov, yeah. Russia was full of them in the 1990s.

MOSLEY: He is such a crook, but you like him as a crook. And the writing is also very funny. One of the great things about your writing is the humor in it.

AKUNIN: It's not serious. Russian literature is so serious.

MOSLEY: I know, right?

AKUNIN: Just think about Russian literature. As a kid, do you want to be the idiot from Dostoevsky, or do you want to be Raskolnikov killing an old lady with an axe? There's just nobody.

MOSLEY: Maybe I can be the Underground Man.

GESSEN: The first Easy book is set in post-war Los Angeles. What drew you to that particular moment?

MOSLEY: People sometimes ask, "How can you write about 1948 when you weren't even born yet?" You're born at a certain time, but then you are raised among people who came much earlier: 1948 was a perfect time for me to write about. When I was seven, eight, nine, ten years old, I was learning about my family, whom I love so much. They were talking about how they acted and what they did and what kind of trouble they got into in 1948, so that was the perfect time.

GESSEN: You started writing these books in the late '80s, right?

MOSLEY: Yeah.

GESSEN: Was the post-war period a time that you felt nostalgic for?

MOSLEY: It's hard to feel nostalgic, being black in America. It's not that you don't like it, or remember it, it's just hard to feel nostalgic for it. "I miss those times when they used to lynch us," and "Those cotton fields were so much fun. I liked going to the special toilets that were made for only me." You don't feel nostalgia. What you do feel, I want to say, is: "I was alive."

I asked my father once, "Dad, were you afraid when you went to World War II?" and he said, "No, I wasn't afraid." And I said, "But you knew it was America fighting the Germans?" He said, "I didn't know I was an American. I got over there, and I said, If the Germans come over to me and say where are the Americans at, well, they're right over there, those white people over there. But instead the Germans started shooting at me. So the Germans taught me I'm an American." Some people haven't experienced this kind of revelation at all.

I love talking about this, because Americans don't know anything about the history of the world. Americans say, "ISIS is evil," and I go, "Okay, but you do remember the Wahhabis in Saudi Arabia?" And they go, "Who? What? Where?" And I say, "You do remember that we hired Iraq to wage war on Iran? Killed over a million people, wounded five million, destroyed a giant part of the world's culture?" And they go, "There was a war between Iraq and Iran?" It's like that. Americans don't know history, Americans aren't taught history, and the history that Americans are taught is a lie. Literature has a lot of work to do in this country.

GESSEN: Boris, you've said something similar, that you had to make Fandorin the opposite of a Russian?

AKUNIN: Not the opposite of a Russian, but someone who possessed the qualities that we lack as a nation. That is why Fandorin is attractive to Russian readers, I think.

MOSLEY: When I read the first book, I was like, "I'm gonna steal this from you." A young person from the upper class who loses all of his money and becomes a detective, with this older guy as his sidekick because the young guy is just so much smarter—I thought this was such a new notion. I was very excited about that. I like turning something on its head.

GESSEN: But Easy Rawlins is a pretty typical guy.

MOSLEY: Well, Ellison's *Invisible Man* is about a black man you can't see. It's a very philosophical novel. Easy is an invisible man because nobody expects a black man at that time to know what's going on. He could be the janitor, he could be the cook, or he could just be passing by. They might be talking, and they'd think, *We're talking smart, so he won't understand what we're saying.* Also in his own community, they'd think, *You're black, so you can't possibly do anything outside of our community.* Everywhere he goes, he is invisible.

GESSEN: In a way, he also feels trapped by his community. Mouse is a person he is trying to get away from all the time, right? But when he is in trouble, he needs Mouse.

MOSLEY: Easy is in trouble because he's made some money, he didn't pay his taxes, and the IRS is after him. Mouse looks at him, and he's like, "Wait a minute. What's wrong?" Easy says, "The IRS is after me." Mouse says, "What's the man's name? I'll kill that motherfucker." Easy says, "Well, if you kill him, there's just gonna be another," and Mouse says, "Well, I'll kill him, too, and then I'll burn down the courthouse, man. All your papers will be gone." That's Mouse, right? Mouse is the guy. Whether Easy is afraid of Mouse or not, he needs him. Mouse says, "Hey, man, them white people got people at their back. You got me." So whether he's upset or not, in the end, he and Mouse are always going to be together. Unless Mouse kills him.

GESSEN: These characters are immensely likable. How do you do that?

AKUNIN: With Erast Fandorin, it's easy. You make him very handsome. He acts nobly, and you make him a bit vulnerable. Fandorin stutters.

MOSLEY: He also lost all his money, right?

AKUNIN: Yeah, and he's foolish when he falls in love. Women love that.

MOSLEY: What you're saying might be true. People come up to me, and they say—women will say, for instance, "I'm really in love with Easy. I want to meet him." They actually say, "I want his phone number." And I say, "His phone number is in the past. I don't know if you can get it." They think he is beautiful, even though I have never described him. It's kind of wild. But one of the great things about writing, about literature itself, is that the readers make up most of the book. If you and I had to describe everything that's going on in this room, it would take us five lifetimes to do that, so we describe a very tiny little bit, and then the audience makes up the rest of it. If you give a couple of hints—a couple of jokes, a couple of beautiful places—then they come in and they make up all the rest. It's the readers.

AKUNIN: And of course we exploit the cinema. You just use your brush to hint at something, and readers have associations with film characters or some TV series. You don't lose momentum, you don't lose speed: You just do a few touches. When Tolstoy had to describe someone, he had to use pages on it.

MOSLEY: It's like reading *Moby-Dick* and thinking, *My God.* I mean, it's a great book, but my god, the amount of description—

AKUNIN: Yeah, it needs an editor, definitely.

MOSLEY: But people were happy then without TV. They didn't have radio. "I'll read this book. I don't have anything else to do. I finished the Bible yesterday, and I'm reading *Moby-Dick* today. Tomorrow I'll read *The Iliad.*"

GESSEN: How has Fandorin changed over the last twenty years?

AKUNIN: What I don't like about Sherlock Holmes or Miss Marple is that they don't change. I wanted to write a saga about a hero who gets older, who makes mistakes, who matures, who evolves. That sort of thing. In the first novel, Fandorin was twenty. In the latest he is almost sixty, and he is very different.

MOSLEY: Yeah, my first Easy is twenty-eight, and in the book I just finished, he is forty-eight. He's getting older, more experienced, changing, seeing the world differently—and the world is changing. That just makes it more interesting for us, right? I'm not writing the same story again and again.

AKUNIN: And you are changing, too, over the years.

MOSLEY: Exactly, exactly.

GESSEN: How do your changes relate to your characters' changes?

AKUNIN: I'm interested in other things. I'm motivated by other things. I'm fascinated by the process of living, generally. I want my character to achieve the impossible, to age beautifully, so that life at sixty will be more shining and fascinating and interesting than life at thirty.

MOSLEY: I'm not arguing with that. That sounds good. I mean, I don't care about my characters. I would like that for me. My characters will lose legs. The portrait of Dorian Gray gets ugly. But, you know, I'll stay young and beautiful.

AKUNIN: We are using them like mice in a laboratory, you know. We try it on them to see what is good for us and what is bad for us.

MOSLEY: Yeah, yeah.

AKUNIN: May I ask you a professional question?

MOSLEY: Yeah.

AKUNIN: Do you read other people's writing? Other people's books? Because I stopped. When I started writing I stopped reading. I discovered it was bad for me.

MOSLEY: I don't read mysteries at all. One day, I had finished writing one of the Easy Rawlins novels, and you know how you talk to yourself and go a little crazy? I thought, *This book seems familiar.* And I said to myself, *Well, of course, fool, you just wrote it.* And I go, *No…* and I remembered I had read another book, and I had used exactly that plot in this book, and I had to go back and rewrite the whole book and change the plot, because it had gone into my unconscious and come out as I was writing. So I stay away from reading mysteries. I can read other things. I read Márquez anytime. I read poetry.

GESSEN: But we know you've been reading each other's books, so we are now going to be looking for—

MOSLEY: I'm going to steal his writing.

AKUNIN: Professional reading spoils everything. You read a novel, and what you think about is how it's done. *Okay. This is good. This is bad. This I can use. This I cannot use.*

MOSLEY: I would love it if you all of a sudden wrote about a black detective in Moscow. That would be so cool.

AKUNIN: I did it once. I wrote a Western once. Fandorin is in America and has a colleague who's black. And who fools him.

MOSLEY: Good.

GESSEN: I haven't read *Charcoal Joe* yet, but in *Rose Gold*, Easy is constantly getting harassed by the police. Every interaction with a white person turns into some kind of problem for him, more so than in the first book.

MOSLEY: Yeah, because in the first book, he is in the black community. After a while, he starts moving out into the larger community, and people are resistant. Especially after the riots. In the '40s, early '50s, all of Easy's work is in the black community. As he gets more well-known, as integration begins to work, he's outside in other places.

I've had people pull guns on me five times in my life. All of them were policemen, and all of them were in Los Angeles, and I was never doing anything wrong. One cop actually took out a gun, pointed it at my balls, and said, "Why did you break into this building?" And I'm sitting there with my father in my head. My father's saying to me, *Walter, if a man has a gun on you, don't you argue with him.* And I'm thinking, *Yeah, but if I say yes, then he's going to take me to jail.* And my father says, *But if you say no, he's going to shoot you.* So I went, "Uh, no, officer, I did not." I said it slowly as if I wasn't disagreeing. "I did not break into that building." It wasn't funny then, but it's funny now: The policemen are stopping you, and the policemen are scared of you. One time I was twelve, and I was on a bicycle. I weighed about eighty pounds. It was 1964, and a policeman said to me, "I'm stopping you because somebody just stole a television set." That was 1964. Even a portable television set weighed forty-five pounds. I said, "Officer, I don't have a television," and he said, "Don't get smart with me." And I'm thinking (I didn't say it), *Well, somebody has to be smart.*

GESSEN: Is there anything in your own thinking that is changing and that makes you want to put Easy in certain situations?

MOSLEY: You asked me if I read. I would come back with a question: Do you think when you write? Because I don't. I don't say, "Oh, I'm going to start writing about Easy Rawlins." I just start writing, and things happen, but I'm not really completely aware of their happening. I certainly don't make plans like that.

AKUNIN: You don't?

MOSLEY: No. I just start writing.

AKUNIN: How is it possible for a detective novel not to have a plan?

MOSLEY: The plan comes after. I write the book, and then I say, "I wonder what the plan should be in this book?"

AKUNIN: Don't you start with a trick?

MOSLEY: With what?

AKUNIN: With a trick. First, you have to think of a trick for a detective novel, and then—

MOSLEY: No, nuh-uh.

AKUNIN: Oh really? How interesting.

GESSEN: In *The Diamond Chariot,* the eleventh in the Fandorin series to be translated into English, there are many references going back to the first and second novels. Did you plan that all out in advance?

AKUNIN: Of course. When I started working on this series, I already knew how many novels would be in it and what each novel was going to be about, and even what the last phrase of every novel would be.

MOSLEY: I just keep writing, keep writing, because I figure if I surprise myself then I'll definitely surprise my readers. I'm a strong believer in the unconscious. I'm writing something, so I must have an intention. I just don't know what that intention is. And it goes on and on and on.

So you don't read, and I don't think.

AKUNIN: How interesting. Because I am a complete control freak and afraid of letting go of anything. So I have to plan. Or maybe just because I grew up in a socialist country, and everything was about the planned economy.

I left Russia because I felt I couldn't write there any longer. Politics became so ugly in 2014 that had I stayed in Russia, I would have had to stop writing and become an activist, which I am not and which I am not good at. I would feel under constant stress because of all the stupid things happening around me. If I wanted to keep my sanity and to go on writing, I had to put some distance between myself and Moscow. That was the reason. I do not go there any longer. I can; I'm not persecuted or anything. It's just not good for my work.

GESSEN: Yet you were quite active politically in the years before you left. When you were going to participate in the protests in 2011, 2012, what did you think of your role as a writer? In Russia, that role has a long and complicated history. How did you place yourself?

AKUNIN: The writer in Russia was always a preacher, teaching people, a prophet. I hated all that. I wanted to just become myself. I wanted to become a private person, an individual. I grew up in a communist country where everything around me was collective, and I hated collectivism completely. I wanted to be by myself. I wanted to write entertaining literature. I wanted to have fun. But you know, that does not work if you have a lot of readers, because people start listening to you. If something bad happens in the country, you cannot afford to keep your mouth shut, because this is also a statement. You have to speak up, otherwise you lose respect for yourself. It's not that I was going to take part in politics to achieve something, I just had no choice.

MOSLEY: One has to believe that because you're writing and you have such a large following inside Russia and out, your work is giving people hope. Not in a specific political way, but in a way that says I can imagine myself, as you imagine yourself, alone with this book, thinking thoughts that are my own and going someplace that's my own.

AKUNIN: Had it been so. Unfortunately, these days, with social networks, you get feedback from your readers on a daily basis. I get lots and lots of responses and letters every day, and the majority of my readers tell me, "We love you as an author, but you are so stupid in politics. Stop doing this. We know what is happening in Russia. Just write for us Fandorian-ites. Don't distract yourself with politics." This is depressing.

MOSLEY: But a lot of times you have an impact on people, and it makes a difference, and they don't know it. When you're reading something, and it's a place you want to go to, and it's a time you want to go to, and there are characters that you love, that fills your life in other ways. Sometimes in ways people don't even know. People follow you for a reason.

AKUNIN: I don't want to teach people anything. I take my readers as my equals, as grown-ups. I respect them. I don't feel as if I am above them.

MOSLEY: We're not teachers. We're writers, and some of our readers are smarter than us.

AKUNIN: Absolutely.

MOSLEY: I agree completely. Hey, go to school if you want to be a teacher.

GESSEN: Okay, over here on this side: Walter, what do you think of America?

MOSLEY: Number one, Americans don't have a history. Number two, the working class of America is about eighty percent of America, even though everybody in America thinks they're middle class. Most of the country has had almost all of their wealth stolen from them. Any wealth that they have can be shown in debt to credit cards, to the mortgage on their house, to their car, to their education, to their kids' education, to their kids' kids' education. It's all debt. All of life is debt. There used to be a time in America when that wasn't true.

And that's not a racial thing. There are issues about race, about all kinds of people of color. The night before last, I was given the honor of being called a Grand Master of the Mystery Writers of America. They've been giving that goddamn award for seventy years. I'm the first person who's not white to get it. Even though Chester Himes came before me. I'm not trying to say there aren't problems with race, but I think there are other large problems in America that people understand even less. That's problematic.

I probably don't have as much trouble with the United States as you have with the structure around Putin. But America does crazy things. I mean, we essentially own the Philippines, and we own Puerto Rico. We have armies fighting all over the world to support the wealth not of the people, but of giant corporations, some of which aren't even owned by America. I have lots of trouble with how we work, how we deal with the world, and I'm not that optimistic either. It's not like I think it's going to change.

I can't live in the United States and think things have been bettered when over the last eleven years, millions of people have been murdered and raped in Congo. I just can't feel good about that. Because I know whatever wealth is being gleaned here is partially being gleaned from there, especially from the minerals that make cell phones.

Has it gotten better here? We have the highest incarceration rate in the world. We have all these people in prison. We have fifty thousand people in prison who are in for life without the possibility of parole, and hardly any of them are murderers. Most of them were dealing drugs. When you look at the pharmaceutical companies, I mean, the drug companies are dealing drugs. Come on now. You got your opiates. It's just that heroin is cheaper than most of the opiates that you buy to kill your pain.

GESSEN: We have more people in prison than Russia does.

AKUNIN: We have a lot of people too. Hundreds of thousands.

GESSEN: In Russia?

AKUNIN: Yeah.

GESSEN: But here more.

MOSLEY: Over two million, yeah. They're coming in and they're going out, and they're coming in and going out. It's crazy.

AKUNIN: At least something is worse here than in Russia.

AUDIENCE: Fandorin is kind of an exceptional character. Is there a place for him in contemporary Russia?

GESSEN: If Fandorin were alive today in Russia, what would he be doing?

AKUNIN: He would be a political activist now. He would be a political activist acting stupidly without any support from the country, like some people I know personally continue to do in Russia, to my respect and admiration.

AUDIENCE: I have a question for Walter Mosley. One of your characters in the story "Equal Opportunity," Socrates Fortlow, was played by Laurence Fishburne in the television film *Always Outnumbered*. Can you speak about what he represents in your body of work?

MOSLEY: Writing about Socrates Fortlow was a lot of fun for me. I live in America, and America defines itself by race. It's just—we do. You can't help it. Even when you're not doing it, you're doing it. I decided I needed to create a black philosopher. So I said, "Where do black men learn most things? In prison. And what is their greatest achievement? Getting out of prison and staying out of prison. And when they do those two things, what can they bring back to the community? What intelligence, what awareness, can they bring to the community to help us move further along?" All of that led to Socrates. Twenty-seven years in prison for a terrible crime he committed. He's in the world now and he's trying to stay separate, but he still has to get involved. Either with the young boy who's in trouble or the friends that come to him and say how can we solve this problem. I wrote it to be a young adult book. Because you know, you can read *Catcher in the Rye*, but the people in the inner city don't understand that shit. It's like, man, he had it made. What's he complaining about? He's got money, he's got a place to live, he's got a car, he got a girlfriend. What's the problem? When you live in the hood, there is a whole different set of problems that you have, and Socrates is created to solve those problems.

AKUNIN: Do you sometimes find yourself unable to finish a book?

MOSLEY: Yeah.

AKUNIN: What do you do then?

MOSLEY: I wait. Answer comes up sooner or later. I'm very confident about that. If I can't get it today then I put it down. If I can't get it tomorrow… sooner or later. Listen, it's like life: You got a problem, you have to have an answer—even if it's shooting yourself in the head. You have to have an answer sooner or later.

AKUNIN: With life it's different, because even if you do not solve the problem, it is only your own problem. If you have an army of readers, they wait for your books.

MOSLEY: I love my readers, but I don't care about them. I write the books to make me happy, and I write the books to say stories, and I know that my readers are all going to have a different takeaway from it. Some of them love it, some of them hate it, some of them say, "What's wrong with you?" I don't really care about that. I only care about Socrates or whomever I am working with at the time, and I worry about how they solve their problems. If they do, then that's good, and if they don't, well, they couldn't solve the problem. Because there are some people you can't save, right?

This transcript is adapted from a conversation at the 2016 PEN World Voices Festival.

From **CHARCOAL JOE**

Walter Mosley

"How you doin', Brother Easy," Mouse greeted.

I stood and we shook hands. We were old-school American men and so did not hug.

"Cain't complain," I said with an irrepressible smile. Even the presence of one of the most dangerous men alive could not extinguish my delight with life. "Have a seat."

My visitors' chairs were made from a yellowish wood that was carved to accommodate the human form.

"Damn, niggah, you done burnt a cross in the white man's lawn an' made him like it," Mouse said as he sat back. Light-skinned and light-eyed, he was wearing a straw-colored suit with a Stetson of a wheat hue, a shirt that might have been dyed in blueberries, white silk socks, and patent leather black shoes.

He crossed one leg over the other and grinned at me.

"It's just an office," I said.

"Ain't another Negro in thirty blocks got an office around here, man. You know you just walk right in the lion's den and say, 'Pussy, lay down or get the hell out.'"

"Whisper with me."

"Tinsford's a good man," Mouse half agreed, "but you the one."

"LaMarque dropped by a few days ago. He said that you, him, and Etta went down to Ensenada to do some fishin'."

"Caught me an honest-to-God swordfish. Eleven foot long. Motherfuckah fought harder than any man I ever killed. Shit. It was easier when I had to bite out that man's windpipe when I was handcuffed behind my back."

Mouse was a colorful man, his beauty defined by the distance one had from him.

"I never knew you to go fishing," I said, in an attempt to lighten our conversation. "Not since we were kids down in Houston."

"Etta wants me to retire."

"Retire?"

Retirement was a huge word for Raymond "Mouse" Alexander. To my knowledge he had not held a legitimate job in all his forty-seven years. He might have pretended to be working for a company he planned to rob. He applied for a few jobs after the one stint in prison he ever served. But Mouse never punched a clock or looked at any man as his boss.

His money-making activities over the previous several years had been working with an international heist ring as a gunman, strong-arm, and wild card when circumstances went south. He did two to three jobs a year and once told me that he made more than the president of Bank of America.

"Yeah," Mouse said, giving me a half shrug. "Etta said that a full-grown man shouldn't be making his family worry so hard when he go off to work. I told her that cops and soldiers do that every day. But she come back sayin' that cops retire after twenty years and I been an outlaw since I was five."

Mouse snickered. The truth is often funny.

It struck me that my lifelong friend might have been there to ask for a job. This notion further diminished my good mood. Both Whisper and Saul had told me that they would not be able to enter a partnership that included Raymond.

"So," I ventured tenuously, "what would you do if you retired? I mean would you take on some other kind of work?"

"I got me quite a pile saved up," he said. "And I been thinkin' about what you did."

"Meaning what exactly?" I can honestly say that at that moment there was no cheer in my heart.

Mouse looked me in the eye and smiled. He was a psychopath who had read maybe three books in his entire life but Raymond knew human nature as well as any psychoanalyst with a lifetime of experience.

I believe he knew what was bothering me and reveled in my discomfort.

"Milo Sweet gonna purchase twelve rental properties for me and hire Fearless Jones to maintain the buildin's and collect the rent. Every unit'll be in Etta's name and I'll sit on the front porch livin' the life of Riley."

It was the best solution that my friend could have come up with. He needed a taxable source of income while Etta, his wife and my onetime lover, had to have a nest egg,

Mouse grinned. A ruby festooned one of his front teeth. There was a thick ring of gold and onyx on the baby finger of his left hand.

Our eyes met again and he waited.

"You the one come to me," I said at last.

"You evah hear of a brother named Charcoal Joe?" Mouse asked.

"Heard of him," I admitted. "I don't really know anything about him though. Plays poker and the horses. Got more luck than a rich man askin' for a bank loan." There were a few darker stories about Joe but I had no facts to credit them.

Mouse smiled again. "You always got the right words, Easy. Even if you don't know a thing, you never say nuthin' wrong."

I nodded, accepting the compliment, and waited.

"Joe's what you call a mastermind. He makes things happen where no one else could see the possibilities. He the one told me that doin' what I did here in L.A. was bound to lead to heartbreak. He connected me with the man in Cincinnati make my work possible all ovah the continent. Joe is connected like a spider on his web. One time there was this dude gunnin' for you—"

"Me?"

"Yeah," Mouse said, "man named Grindman, Cully Grindman. He'd been hired by another man, a man named Bashir. Anyway, Grindman asked a waitress in a restaurant near your old office if she ever saw you in there, said you was an old friend and he wanted to say hi. That was Stella Rogers. She aksed one of Joe's people if she should get involved. Joe turned around and told me—now Grindman and Bashir in a graveyard out in East L.A. sharin' space with Sadie and Tesser Klieger."

Mouse was pretty good with words, too. Bonnie had a friend who worked with her as a stewardess on Air France, Ojayit Nadkarni. Ojayit's fiancé had beaten her twice and so she needed to get away. I got Jackson Blue to get her work on one of P9's company jets. She took the job and moved to Chicago.

I thought that was the end of it.

"So you see," Mouse continued, "in a way Charcoal Joe done saved your life."

"Grindman was a hit man?"

"Yes he was."

I didn't need to ask why Mouse hadn't come to me with this information. For him killing was simply a tool of the trade, hardly worth discussing. And we were friends. Where we came from this was the kind of thing that one friend did for the other.

"And what can I do for Mr. Joe?" I asked.

"Last night a white man named Peter Boughman and some other guy called Ducky were shot dead in a house down on the beach at Malibu. Ducky was killed outright and Boughman was tortured before they shot him in the eye and the heart."

"And Joe is involved?"

"Not directly. But he has a friend who has a son who went to that house, by accident, and fount the body. His bad luck was that somebody heard the shot and called the police, who got there before Seymour, Joe's friend's son, could call them himself."

"Seymour what?"

"Brathwaite. Dr. Seymour Brathwaite."

"I thought you said he was a kid?"

"Twenty-two-year-old doctor of physics. Doin' what they call postgraduate work at UCLA."

"White guy?"

"Not unless Sidney Poitier's a white guy."

"And what's in it for your friend Joe?"

"What was in it for him when he saved your ass?"

"The police arrested this kid?"

Mouse nodded.

"They book him for murder?"

"Yes, sir."

"So what can I do?"

"There wasn't no gun."

"They arrested him for what then?"

"Murder, conspiracy, breaking and entering, and resisting arrest."

"Again, what does Joe want from me?"

"He wants to talk to you about the circumstances of the case and to hire you to do what he needs done."

"Like put a couple of bodies in the Jewish graveyard in East L.A.?"

"Naw, Easy, he know that ain't your speed."

"If he doesn't want me to break the law, what does he want?"

"Whatever you ain't got words for you got a question, Ease. I'm tellin' you that my friend wants to meet with you and talk with you about a friend's son been arrested for murder. Ain't no question to that."

"When can I see him?"

"Tomorrow out in Venice."

"Why not today if he's so worried?"

"He's in the Avett Detainment Facility out there. The next visitors' day is tomorrow. Hours start at eleven."

"What's he in jail for?"

"'Bout two months ago a man saw Joe's automobile and made what the lawyer called a disparaging remark about its color, which was brown. Joe's reply was two shots over the man's head. They arrested him for discharging a firearm within city limits. He got around ninety days."

I was silent for the moment, biding my time. I couldn't say no to Mouse. He'd saved my life and had put his on the line for me many times. He was mostly evil and definitely a killer but black men in America had learned centuries ago that the devil not only offered the best deals—he was the only deal in our part of town.

"All right," I said after the proper pretense of waiting. "I'll go down there in the morning. Who should I ask for?"

"Rufus Tyler. Prisoner number six-two-seven-three-one-one-L."

While I wrote down the name and number Mouse pulled a thick wad of cash from his breast pocket; this he placed on my cherry-wood desk.

I looked down at the wad and asked, "What's this?"

"Fi'e thousand dollars."

"Give it back to Joe," I said. "I haven't agreed to take the case yet."

"This money is from me, Easy. I'm the one hirin' you."

"Cheddar or blue?" I asked, taking the cash.

"Say what?"

"I just wanna know what kind of cheese is in this trap."

MY HANDS ARE MY HEART

Gabriel Orozco with Colm Tóibín

COLM TÓIBÍN: While the rest of us were sleeping this morning, I wonder if you'd tell us what you were doing.

GABRIEL OROZCO: I was watching the soccer match. Leicester and Manchester United. I've loved football since I was a kid, I've played it all my life, still love it, and now my son is eleven years old, he loves soccer too, so we share that passion. We like to play together.

TÓIBÍN: Could you talk about how that idea of the ball, the game, the movement, the space, might have mattered to you, might have actually entered into the spirit of your work?

OROZCO: Is this an exam, or something? First grade, or second grade?

TÓIBÍN: No, it's PhD level.

OROZCO: PhD level. About balls.

Well, I still have drawings from when I was a kid. I was fascinated by planets and astronomy. I don't know if it was the influence of man going to the moon when I was about seven, but I remember being fascinated by all those asteroids and planets, and I was drawing them. I was also drawing cars. I always liked cars and speed. And I was fascinated by sports like volleyball and soccer—to just run around the ball and do things with it.

TÓIBÍN: When you were starting to think about making art, what images were you seeing?

OROZCO: I admired Picasso from the very beginning. The Olympic Games were in Mexico in 1968 and I still have some little drawings I did. I was drawing athletes running and jumping, and I drew them Picasso-style. I had a poster of *Guernica* in my room, and I was just trying to draw like Picasso when I was six.

I remember an exhibition of Paul Klee at the Museum of Modern Art in Mexico, and Vasarely, I love Vasarely. My father was a painter, and he was close to the muralists, so I admired Siqueiros, Rivera, and José Clemente Orozco. I grew up looking at murals, looking at art. Early on, I liked waking up in the morning, making drawings and paintings. Wherever I went, from exhibitions in Mexico City to my father's library, I was looking at things. I had quite an early visual education in arts, and I liked it. So I was doing my own research. This was during the Cold War. I grew up in a very political family, from the Left, and American art was not so well-considered. I think I was looking more to German Expressionists, obviously Picasso, Joan Miró, Catalan painting in general, but not so much American art. That came later, mostly through John Cage. I got interested after I finished school and went to Spain. I started to read some things about John Cage and then I got more interested in American art.

TÓIBÍN: Tell us about your father.

OROZCO: My father was a painter. He was part of the third generation of muralist painters, called Escuela Mexicana de Pintura, so his work was figurative, politically oriented, and close to Siqueiros. He worked with Siqueiros on murals. He did murals on buildings in Xalapa, Veracruz, Mexico City, and he painted all his life. He was of the same generation of painters who were later my teachers in the academy. That generation in Mexico was divided between more abstract art, which was considered bourgeois, and the leftist, more politically engaged figurative painting. I grew up in that atmosphere.

My father's studio was in our house, so I watched him paint all the time. I remember going to school, coming back right before lunch, going upstairs, where he was painting. Then I would take my little toys and things and start to paint my toys, or I would start to draw with him. Then we would have lunch, and then he kept painting, all afternoon. So I grew up playing with his paintings. My house was surrounded by writers, musicians, photographers... I was surrounded by artists all the time.

Politically, Mexico City was quite hot in the '60s. A lot of things happened: '68 was the massacre with the students, the world was divided because of the Cold War, and the Communist Party was not legal. Most of the artists were communists, in fact. Since the muralist tradition, they were part of the Communist Party, struggling to get democracy, to improve situations, so it was important. They were definitely engaged.

TÓIBÍN: Was there a time when that changed?

OROZCO: The strategies of political activism or politically engaged work, or how you politically show your opinion, have changed. Now it is more complex. And technology has changed. But I think the political position of the artist always permeates the work in some way. The way it's produced, the way it's distributed, and the way the artist lives. Think about the strategies of the artists in the '60s and the '70s, the movements in France in '68, what was happening in New York, what was happening in England, then in the Eastern Bloc, and how the exchange of political propaganda through art was a kind of confrontation. If you look at all the transitions since the '60s and '70s, you can see that the way politics works in the art is much more complex and diverse.

The first time I left Mexico was in '77, to go to the Soviet Union for summer camp. My father was a member of the Communist Party, which doesn't exist anymore. At that time, as there were Boy Scouts, there were also Pioneers. It was the same, but red. All the Leftist people got invited to go to these camps in Orlyonok or in Artek, camps near the Black Sea, and kids went there for a month at a time. In '72, during the Olympics in Germany, there were mini-Olympics. You would just learn things, go camping, play sports. No weapons, no demonstrations or taking over embassies. This was for kids. It was the things Boy Scouts do, but with a different uniform.

TÓIBÍN: Was there another trip outside Mexico that made a big difference to you?

OROZCO: The most important trip I took around then was probably Paris five years later. I went for the first time, and I remember arriving and being so impressed by the city... I've been in love ever since. I always go back there. Just to see such a city, to see the people in the street walking like that… Mexico was different, quite an isolated country in many ways.

After finishing at the academy, I moved to Spain, and that was very important, too. They had just opened the Reina Sophía Museum, and the library was new and wonderful. They were translating a lot of books about European art and American art into Spanish, and there were many new publications. Spain was opening up after Franco. It was the time of the Movida Madrileña, and they had just built this new museum. I was there for one year. I took some workshops, but since I didn't have that much money, I just started to do things in the street, walking toward the workshop or around my house, and then reading a lot. There were some shows, but I mostly learned through books.

Before arriving in Spain, I read a lot of semiotics because of my dissertation in school in Mexico. I was interested in semiotics, in Roland Barthes, Umberto Eco, and Louis Marin. I tried to make my dissertation about one painting I was doing, analyzing it through semiotics, trying to think of painting as a language form.

TÓIBÍN: What novels have influenced you?

OROZCO: Novels don't really appeal to me. I like semiotics, I like philosophy, I like technical books. Also stories.

Through philosophy I got into Borges. In Mexico, you read Borges in school. I wasn't so engaged by him at the beginning, but after coming out of semiotics and linguistics and philosophy, to find a writer who was playing with language in a way that made everything science fiction, even philosophy as a branch of science fiction? "The Aleph" was important to me—many, many short stories by Borges were. He gave me a lot of room to think in a way that was not so academic. In Spain I read him all the time. Suzuki on Zen Buddhism was also influential. And I discovered John Cage during that time.

There was a lovely book published in Spain by a Spanish musician who told the story of John Cage. He talks about chance operations and Zen Buddhism in Cage's work. At that time, I was not even that interested in listening to the music. A few years later, I met John Cage and I listened to him at concerts in New York, but in 1986 it was more about finding a technique that included chance, accident, noise, non-coded sound.

After reading Cage, and after looking at things and doing things in Spain that were not about painting, but more about objects in the streets and things like that, I came back to Mexico and started to do the same kinds of things around my house in the south of the city. Then I did an exhibition with objects and installation work at a very outsider place, an empty ex-convent which became a kind of cultural house on the city's outskirts, on the mountain in the Desierto de los Leones. I organized a group show with other artists. In a little empty chapel, I put up a big elephant head in place of the cross, and I put some wood from an old dead tree on the floor, so the tree trunks and the elephant looked like they were from the same body, and they were in this Catholic space.

TÓIBÍN: How has Catholicism influenced your work?

OROZCO: Obviously Catholicism is part of my culture, and there are things in my art you can think are connected to that, but I wasn't really raised as a Catholic, and there are things about Catholicism in art that I don't like much. Even muralism was too Catholic for me. It had some kind of didactic, preaching imagery that was close to the Renaissance style, and to the vision of the Western world in the Catholic way. All things I try not to do. So putting the elephant head there was more about the idea of martyrdom, or the idea of an animal, a dead animal. The whole thing was, in a way, mystical. People got offended.

TÓIBÍN: When did you start taking photographs?

OROZCO: Some of my friends were interested in photography, and the mother of one of my best friends is an important photographer. Around '85 there was a big earthquake in Mexico City, and after the earthquake, we went out. We helped people as much as we could, but the city was so transformed, and was quite intense. We wanted to document that. So I became more active, taking photos. I didn't own a camera, but I borrowed one. I took photos of some people, but I felt really uncomfortable taking portraits, especially of people in a state of vulnerability. Since then, I have tried to focus on objects, on things that definitely bear the presence of the human body or the drama of life, or whatever you want to call it, but not of private personal life.

I got my first camera myself around '91. I bought a Nikon autofocus, and then I started to use it more and more because it was small, it fit in my pocket. Photography became part of everyday life.

"SLEEPING DOG"

This photo was taken with the camera I borrowed. It's a sleeping dog. I approached the dog—I saw it on the beach. It was almost vertical, and I was fascinated because it looked like it was floating. It's so vulnerable but peaceful. It looks dead somehow, but it's just sleeping. I took the photo and I left. This photo became important to me because it represents contact with the world in terms of gravity, sculpture, tenderness, discovery, connection.

When I started to work with found things, there was always a question about transportation. Transporting things was expensive in Mexico, and transporting them out was even more expensive, so I tried to make work that I could transport myself. For a few years, from '86 until '92, I was just transporting my work myself. So I did work that fit in my luggage. Portability became an important consideration, and the idea of transport became important, too. The mobility of the work as part of the work, not accessory. Photography became important because I could do big things in the landscape, I didn't need to transport them. Photography became a transportation system for my work.

But then, I also did the inflatable rubber ball and the plasticine ball. It was all about moving and transport, strength and vulnerability, and accepting the inevitability of constant movement. At that time, I was not using the studio much. I was more interested in working in the streets, finding objects instead of producing inside a space. Since then, I haven't used studios that much.

Sleeping Dog, 1990
Silver dye bleach print
20 × 16 in. / 50.8 × 40.6 cm
Courtesy of the Artist and
Marian Goodman Gallery

"Crazy Tourist"

This was taken in Cachoeira, in the north of Brazil. Suddenly, around six, the market was ending, people were leaving, and there was this bunch of oranges in a corner. They were all broken, so they were useless. The light was so beautiful, the whole thing was special. I put one or two on the table because it was especially bright, to see the orange. It's not a fancy photo; the definition is quite poor. Anyway, I just put oranges around the market. There were a couple of drunk guys on the left, and they were saying, "Turista maluco, tan maluco," which is "Crazy Tourist," the title of the work. This is '91, when I was living in Brazil. At that opening in Mexico, I had met a beautiful woman, we fell in love, then she became my girlfriend. She liked to travel a lot, and then I had to follow her, because if not…

We went to Brazil together, happily, and it was really very important, because the physicality of the landscape there is quite different from Mexico, the sculptural tradition is very different. Everything is so different. Language, sound, everything. We spent time in the north, Salvador de Bahia, Rio de Janeiro, and those six months in Brazil were very productive. I became curious about Cildo Meireles, Waltércio Caldas, Tunga, and the work of that generation.

We spent six months in Brazil, then came back to Mexico. Before that, I'd come to New York a couple of times. In 1980, for example, I came to see the Picasso show at MoMA; since then I come every two or three years to see shows here. I come to hear music, to go to concerts and things. I remember enjoying the "Water Lilies" of Monet in MoMA, very much, for example. That room was important, "Water Lilies," that work, Monet's work was so important in founding the museum, the beginnings of MoMA. The connection with that work is very important.

The time when you could actually have a room to have privacy to enjoy

Crazy Tourist, 1991
Chromogenic color print
16 × 20 in. / 40.6 × 50.8 cm
Courtesy of the Artist and
Marian Goodman Gallery

Extension of Reflection, 1992
Chromogenic color print
16 × 20 in. / 40.6 × 50.8 cm
Courtesy of the Artist and
Marian Goodman Gallery

a work of art is gone. There is not such a space or time. My work now has to deal with that. It's not so much about having the space for art, because there are many spaces for art, but about having the time for art. How you can have the time to actually see the work. That doesn't exist anymore. I was not so much into galleries, I have to say, I just went to the museums. I was going to the Metropolitan, to the Frick. I was interested in music, so it was nice to go to some concerts, and even CBGB, I remember going there very young. Buying music at Tower Records.

"EXTENSION OF REFLECTION"

This was one of the first works I made here. It was my bicycle on the East River side, right after a rain shower. I was just riding my bike, and suddenly I started to go around the puddles. I noticed that all the bikers were avoiding puddles.

At that time, I was thinking about chance, accident, unpredictability, topology, and how the grid is always accident by accident by accident, accentuated by different phenomena that break the geometry or the structure of the urban and the organized. I thought, *Well, why not go through the puddles instead of trying to avoid them, and go in circles?* Then I did this work. And I was happy with it. When I was doing it, I didn't realize the reflection of the sky was in the puddles. Then I stepped off my bike, and quickly took the photo (because it was drying out), and then I saw the reflection of the sky. The title of the work is "Extension of Reflection."

"DIAL TONE"

This was in 1992. When I was in New York at that time, the first thing I had in my apartment was a telephone and the phone book, and it was

Dial Tone, 1992
Cut-and-pasted phone book
pages on Japanese paper
11" × 34'/27.9 × 1.036 cm
Courtesy of the Artist and
Marian Goodman Gallery

Yielding Stone, 1992
Plasticine
14 × 17 × 17 in. / 35.6 × 43.2 × 43.2 cm
Courtesy of the Artist and
Marian Goodman Gallery

otherwise empty. I thought, *This book is strange*. I took out all the names, and left just the columns with numbers. Somehow, the idea was to try to make a musical score out of the complete set of numbers of telephones in New York. So I started to do that, column by column, and I cut the whole phone book. This work is twenty-five meters long.

"YIELDING STONE"

This is the plasticine ball. It's my weight in plasticine, which is this material used for modeling and sculpture, but normally it's not the material that you use for the finished work. I was working with that, and somehow, I couldn't do anything I liked. Then I liked seeing how it gets dirty, and it's always soft. I decided to make my weight in a big chunk of plasticine and then roll it in the street. I call it "Yielding Stone," the idea of the stone that is always vulnerable, always changing, always receiving accidents. Yes, it's a body, and it's my body in a way. It's formless, but it's always transforming.

"LA DS"

In '93, I did this piece, because I was talking about cutting and imploding space, and then about transportation and speed and the dynamic of perspective in space and time. I bought an abandoned Citroën DS outside Paris. The idea was to cut it from the axle of the steering wheel and the other side, exactly the same measurement, and then rejoin them again. Obviously the engine is gone. It was done by hand, so we had to do one piece at a time, different materials by hand or with different tools, depending on the material, and then it was joined together and painted. Two of us worked on this for one month in a garage. It's not so different from when people do custom things for their cars.

La DS, 1993
Modified Citroën DS
55-3/16" × 15'9-15/16" × 45-5/16" /
140.1 × 482.5 × 115.1 cm
Courtesy of the Artist and Galerie
Chantal Crousel, Paris

Four Bicycles (There is Always One Direction), 1994
Bicycles
6'6" × 4" × 7'4". / 198.1 × 223.5 × 223.5 cm
Courtesy of the Artist and
Marian Goodman Gallery

"FOUR BICYCLES"

This is "Four Bicycles (There Is Always One Direction)." I did it in Rotterdam. It's important to work with the material you find in a place. My rule was if I was going out to do work in the street or traveling, I should not have with me any material that would imply that I would have to use it. So then with traveling or being outside, it had to be with something I found onsite. I was in Rotterdam for an exhibition, and then I started to work with these bicycles.

"EMPTY SHOE BOX"

I was in the Venice Biennale, and I was invited into the Aperto. There was this small space, and a big row with all these boots. Working with specificity, I decided to show this shoebox. It was not protected. The curator was worried it was going to be destroyed, but I said, "If you glue it to the floor, that's worse, because if people kick it, it's going to be destroyed. It's better if they kick it and it's just moving around." Fifteen minutes before the opening, they took it out because they thought it was trash…but I have my suspicion it was another jealous artist. I had to get another shoebox. I didn't buy the shoes, because I was very convincing that I only needed the shoebox. I got plenty more to keep backstage, because they would disappear. I showed it in Venice, empty like that, with the top on the bottom like that, and it became a really important piece for me. About transportation, emptiness, vulnerability, all those subjects that are somehow constant in my work.

Empty Shoe Box, 1993
Shoe box
4-7/8 × 13 × 8-1/2 in. /
12.4 × 33 × 21.6 cm
Installation view of 45th International
Art Exhibition: The Cardinal Points
of Art, Venice Biennale, 1993
Courtesy of the Artist and
Marian Goodman Gallery

Empty Shoe Box, 1993
Silver dye bleach print
16 × 20 in. / 40.6 × 50.8 cm
Courtesy of the Artist and
Marian Goodman Gallery

"HOME RUN"

This is the orange. It was a project for MoMA. I did some things in the building, I showed "The Yielding Stone" and other works, but then I wanted to work outside, because it seemed logical: Obviously, you have oranges in the apartments. The museum liked the idea, and we provided oranges to the neighbors in front. They were using the oranges for orange juice, then replacing them with new oranges in the window, and you could see this from the museum. The idea of public art, probably coming from this idea of muralism or art in public spaces, was and is important to me. This was a different way of doing muralism, maybe, or a different way of approaching or appropriating this space between private and public, the museum and the street, the private lives in the apartments and the public life in a museum. It's called "Home Run." Just imagine all the buildings with different oranges in all the windows, for twelve floors.

"MY HANDS ARE MY HEART"

I made the work out of brick clay, so it's very porous. It's solid. It's a sculpture made with hands and clay. Classic, and very simply made. Then I took photographs of the work and it did not look good. Somehow it was hard to make clear what the object was. Then at some point a friend was helping me, and we developed the idea of this diptych, because then you could see the process of the work, and also understand the piece. (See cover illustration.) Obviously, it's the size of my hands, it was me, and I had just made it. Somehow, I am the base of the sculpture. The sculpture is there; I'm the base. This coming from the body has been important in my work: representing the actions of the body and the scale of the body in relation to landscape or nature or materials.

Home Run, 1993
Oranges
Dimensions variable
Installation views of Projects 41: Gabriel Orozco,
The Museum of Modern Art,
New York, 1993
Courtesy of the Artist and Marian Goodman Gallery

"YOGURT CAPS"

This is '94, my first show in New York, at Marian Goodman Gallery. I showed four yogurt lids, one on each wall of the gallery. Just four. Obviously, it was very hard to take a photo of all four at once. It's just the plastic tops of the yogurt. They don't make them anymore. Now they are collector's items, these things. Very hard to find. Marian Goodman came to the gallery, saw this, and then she saw the show, and I was like, "Hey, how about this?" And she was like, "Well, Gabriel, you still have time to think of something else." This was three days before the opening.

The day of the opening, I decided yes, to go for it, and at the very beginning, people were arriving, and then immediately turning around and going out. They were not even sure there was a show. Then people started to come back, and slowly entered the space, as if it had been closed, and at first they couldn't get in, but then suddenly they could. They realized it was empty but it was not really empty. You have these blue rings on exactly the opposite four points of the four walls, and you are moving, and they start to move, even if you don't realize they are: You became the center point or the centrifugal point of the space, just because you have the reference. You start to move, and then the work starts to move. Then you go closer and you see what it is, it's just a yogurt lid. There's no mystery, except why they are there and how they behave when you are there. Which is similar to what happened with the shoebox. It's a shoebox, but then your behavior starts to change as much as the behavior of space of the shoebox and what it is in terms of reality, art, sculpture, whatever. It starts to change. So that's what happened with the work.

Yogurt Caps, 1994
Four yogurt lids
Each: 3-1/8 in. diam. / 7.9 cm diam.
Installation view at Marian Goodman
Gallery, New York, 1994
Courtesy of the Artist and
Marian Goodman Gallery

Yogurt Caps (detail), 1994
One of four yogurt lids
Each: 3-1/8 in. diam. / 7.9 cm diam.
Courtesy of the Artist and
Marian Goodman Gallery

"Sand on Table"

It's on the beach, in Mexico, in Oaxaca, and these are the classic tables you have in the little cabaña restaurants with the fishermen, somehow so banal, and the gesture is so banal, almost like a kid would throw sand on the top of a table, just until it gets filled, and you cannot fit more sand. That's exactly the limit of the surface. Reflecting about sculpture, the floating world, why we put things on a table—and I have many working tables—you raise something from the floor to have it on the table because it's something precious for you or it's something you want to use in some way. So this is very simple, and it's all very common, but then perhaps it's precisely like the shoebox. It's there in a way that you think about the void, the moment, gravity, in terms of sculpture, in terms of time, or in terms of the sands of the desert. There's something mythological—or maybe just banal.

FROM THE INSTALLATION "Visible Labor"

These are pieces of Buddhist temples. I was interested in the joinery system, how they build up temples and houses in Japan, and I mixed that with the go games, so it's also this kind of chess about territory, but I expanded on the whole installation, and in every piece I put some red Ferraris and some Buddhas. Again, I guess this idea of the empty space that joins. Basically, an empty space is a space to be occupied, and that space is a space of connection with something. The void, emptiness. I painted in white the area of the joinery.

Sand on Table, 1992
Silver dye bleach print
16 × 20 in. / 40.6 × 50.8 cm
Courtesy of the Artist and
Marian Goodman Gallery

IGO-KIGUMI/BUDDHA/FERRARI, 2015
Acrylic on wood, Buddha figures, miniature
car models, Go board game and stones
Dimensions variable
Installation at Rat Hole Gallery, Tokyo,
2015–2016
Courtesy of the Artist and
Marian Goodman Gallery

AUDIENCE: Word, image, and imagination: How do you connect the three?

OROZCO: The whole philosophical Western world was based on this question! It's a fundamental question. I should ask this myself every day, every morning!

You just start to walk. You just start your day. You wake up in the morning and it's not like you say, "Oh, I'm going to fall in love today," because if you look for it, you probably won't find it. But then another day, you just start to walk, then you fall in love. Provoking those situations is difficult, because you need to be empty, relaxed, open to whatever happens, with no prejudice. And then imagination starts to happen. And then communication starts to happen. And language, and image, and all that… You just understand what you are open to understand. So when you can clean yourself and empty yourself of prejudice, you can just start your walk, or your journey, or your day, and then find something that you think is your imagination, but no, it's real. And then you fall in love, and then you can generate some sign to communicate that.

This transcript is adapted from a conversation at the 2016 PEN World Voices Festival.

EAST TEXAS MACHINERY

Gene Walker

His laugh was one of Mel Blanc's many characters, a Woody Wood-pecker rapid-fire repetition of coughs, laughs, and spasms, like he was constantly exhaling a deep bong hit, seduced by the blue-gray vapor invading his brain. It was all due to a vicious case of asthma. At night he was connected to a breathing machine and during the day a tiny plastic inhaler. It was exhausting just trying to talk to him. When he got excited, his laugh would turn into coughs and then to spasms, which had the puzzling effect of making him laugh that much harder. He was back and forth to the hospital weekly with tales of "them letting him die again." It was, understandably, the center of his existence, this bitter respiratory illness, but he wheezed and coughed his way into my life with his quirky toothless smile, crazy laugh, and all the frenetic energy of a penniless crack addict at the break of dawn, searching for a cigarette and a deep, sizzling hit from his glowing pipe.

A bantamweight white guy, not an ounce more than 145 pounds, he was as battered as an old West Texas Ford pick-up, sandblasted then baked with a petroleum stink. He was covered with the indecipherable gibberish of fifty fading, unfinished tattoos, momentary fragments of his life—another skin on top of his own. The three-inch screw scrawled on his forehead, blood dripping from the impact, attested to his life better than any of the others: screwed. He confessed to me once that his pa used to beat him. His father claimed it was to "Rebuke and Banish the Devil." But as he entered the nebula of puberty, the only one banished was him. He would pass out on the floor or the yard and wake to his dog licking him on the face. One day he just stopped going home and started hustling with his body. Men, women. It didn't matter. It wasn't about the sex, it was about the money. Survival. He had long ago detached himself from his vessel. It was now just an instrument. A means to an end. He was a butterfly separated from his wings, condemned to a worm's-eye view. His essence was altered, redefined, but his new tool paid for the smokes, for the food, and for a string of twenty-minute highs that became his life.

It is the endless refrain of our songs: "No, he was not always like this." None of us was. But life unfolds in staggering diversity and randomness. Cruel, beautiful, and indifferent, it is a great ocean of contradictions, and we are conscious from incision to suturing. His name was Mark, and we called him Cowboy.

This past August, "those people" did let him die when they refused to treat him for an asthma attack. He stumbled into medical, shouting, "I can't breathe… I'm dying, you stupid motherfuckers!" He was delirious and terrified and refused to leave medical, begging them to get him to a hospital. He was summarily handcuffed in what's called a "Flash" and taken off to a solitary cell for failing to obey an order. It is an efficient ritual, executed hundreds of times a day in prisons in Texas. But this time, he did die. He suffocated in the heat of the heavy August air, choking on the gasps and spasms in the empty chasm of his lungs. It is a crime many men here will do ten to fifteen years for: negligent homicide. A watered-down murder charge, but murder just the same. Doctors do it, surgeons, neglectful parents—it's when you kill someone by not doing something. Murder without the intent. Intent is the determinant in these things. This is the kind of murder they let you apologize for. You do a suspended five-year sentence. You keep your house and your wife, your clothes. But the other sucker, he loses everything.

He lies now in a tiny grave dug out then refilled some moments later by men in white. The unit chaplain makes a short petition to the Father to accept his Soul into Heaven and to forgive him his sins. It, like the Flash, is just another ritual here, mandated by a Policy & Procedure Manual in a Director's office and executed in an emotionless manner by an employee whose actions are defined and dictated to be just another part of a larger apparatus. I suppose we are lucky if the chaplain even knows our names. Maybe then he will make an actual, more personal appeal for us. "We were not always…" Even here, a tradition is not without its obligations.

His mail is not marked "Deceased." He did not make the obituaries column in the local paper. No blank stare from a one-inch-square picture from when he still had teeth or hair, before his wings were plucked in flight. No, none of that. Just his unclaimed property, a ravaged body in a painted wooden coffin milled from the tall pines of this East Texas machinery. It never blinks.

Gene Walker won first place in essay in PEN America's 2016 Prison Writing Contest.

PRISON BRANDING IN
THE AGE OF MASS INCARCERATION

During the 2016 PEN World Voices Festival, the PEN Prison Writing Committee and The Writer's Foundry gave a multimedia presentation investigating the corporate side of our prison-industrial complex. Helen Hofling, coordinator of The Writer's Foundry, and Timothy Small, coordinator of the PEN Prison Writing Program, focused their scrutiny on CCA, the largest private corrections company in the United States, and the corporation's attempts to use language to sanitize its image.

Hofling writes of the CCA website's labyrinthine structure:

CCA stands for the Corrections Corporation of America. The full name is hard to find on their website, despite the considerable volume of text published there... CCA's branding mechanism features an impressive array of smiling, diverse faces in and out of uniform; dramatic tales of volunteerism; ethical assurances; value guarantees; video clips with exhilarating soundtracks; promises of meaningful careers; and outlines of comprehensive rehabilitation programming. The impression they give is of a midsize liberal arts college or a particularly well-funded organization dedicated to public works.

CCA makes their case for the public good: "We benefit America by protecting public safety, employing the best people in solid careers, preparing inmates for reentry, giving back to communities, and bringing innovative security to government corrections—all while consistently saving hardworking taxpayers' dollars. We are America's Leader in Partnership Corrections."

They invoke America, with the adjectives "best," "solid," "innovative," and "hardworking." Page headings include "Protecting Inmate and Detainee Rights," "Adding Value for Taxpayers," "Providing Proven Reentry Programs," "Improving our Communities," "Ensuring Governance with

Integrity," and "Fostering Meaningful Careers." Each of these pages has subpages and sub-subpages that open and shut like a telescope or a family of nesting dolls: resources, PDFs, and links to "news" articles that circle back to the CCA website. The themes of these categories hop back and forth: inmates to taxpayers, them to us, reentry to communities.

The notion of "proven results" is repeated several times, though what these results are, or how they have been proven, is not remarked upon. My efforts to sketch a boundary of understanding around CCA.com are continually frustrated. Though this is a self-contained world, kaleidoscopically referring to its own moving interior parts and devoid of external links, the seemingly authorless (or collectively authored) website knows no perimeter, and only invites duplication. The rhetorical apparatus is so successful that I cannot distinguish among what is being concealed, revealed, and constructed.

Timothy Small examines the corporation's representation of itself in its report to shareholders:

To reinforce its role as a public servant, the word "private" is almost entirely omitted from the report. It appears just three times. The word "partner," however, appears forty-one times: *"We see our government partners facing serious challenges"; "CCA has a clear commitment to our government partners"; "We've taken what we've learned in more than thirty years serving our government partners…"*

By the end of the report, CCA has referred to its "government partners" so many times one has a hard time remembering that CCA is not part of the government, nor is the government part of CCA; the government is CCA's client.

Despite CCA's proclaimed commitment to *reduce* recidivism, *lower* the cost of incarceration, *save* taxpayers money, *alleviate* overcrowding, *break* the cycle of crime, *expansion,* not *reduction,* seems to be their focus. In just twelve pages of text, the words "expansion" (or some variation), "build," "construct," "rise," "acquire," "develop," "increase," "extend," "span," and "ramp" are used seventy times. In every context, it is the measure of *growth,* celebrated as an "achievement," a "success," a "highlight," or a "meaningful contribution."

This is not a distortion: Even as the inmate population in federal facilities has declined over the past two years, CCA has continued to expand. In 2015, it constructed new facilities, renewed state and federal contracts, and increased its revenue by 8.9 percent. How can this be? How can expansion and reduction occur simultaneously?

How many people in CCA's custody have successfully reintegrated into society? How many people *did not* return to prison after their release? Can expansion and reduction really be simultaneous? What happens to the manufactures of blood sugar test strips if diabetes is cured? Or to the makers of armor if there are no wars? Can a for-profit prison be truly invested in the permanent release and rehabilitation of inmates without also being invested in its own collapse?

Since this presentation took place the corporation has rebranded itself as *CoreCivic*. To learn more, visit their website at www.corecivic.com.

NARRATIVE ANIMALS

Salman Rushdie with Lila Azam Zanganeh

LILA AZAM ZANGANEH: When I was about fourteen years old in Paris, I did a presentation on *The Satanic Verses*—I never thought that someday I'd be sitting here interviewing Salman myself!

To begin, let's talk about how English becomes inhabited by other languages, by other imaginaries. A few years ago, in *The Paris Review,* you talked about your memories of India, and also languages. Originally your family was from Kashmir, but you came from a part of India where both Urdu and Hindi were spoken.

SALMAN RUSHDIE: I grew up in Bombay, where there are a lot of languages. I invented this acronym for the five main languages, HUG ME: Hindi, Urdu, Gujarati, Marathi, English.

ZANGANEH: Hindustani is a combination—?

RUSHDIE: Hindustani is a mixture of Hindi and Urdu, and it is what almost everyone speaks, although it doesn't really exist. It's also the language of the movies.

ZANGANEH: Of Bollywood.

RUSHDIE: Yeah, except that's a newish word, "Bollywood," and I'm not very fond of it. They were just Bombay movies when I was growing up. In Bombay, movies are everywhere. They obsess people in a way that's impossible to explain. Movies were my first cultural influence; books came much later.

ZANGANEH: The first time you ever wrote was after seeing *The Wizard of Oz*.

RUSHDIE: It had songs, and fairies and witches: It was like a Bombay movie translated into English. I must have been eight or nine or maybe ten, and I went home and wrote a short story called "Over the Rainbow." It wasn't about the world of Oz; it was about a boy like myself walking down a street of my hometown and seeing the beginning of the rainbow arching up. The rainbow, rather usefully, had rainbow-colored steps cut into it, so you could go over the rainbow. The little boy in the story makes this journey and meets all kinds of creatures.

I gave the story to my father, who was very proud of it, and he got his secretary to type it up. It was five or six pages. Then my father said, "If I give it to you, you'll lose it, so I'll look after it." Then *he* lost it. That's probably a very good thing.

There's another lost text. I went home to see my parents after leaving boarding school, which I hated. I already had a place at Cambridge, but I didn't want to go. Eventually they persuaded me, and I had a much better time, but in that four or five months between finishing school and going to university, I wrote a novel called *Terminal Report*.

ZANGANEH: Which was thinly veiled autobiography.

RUSHDIE: It was ridiculously thinly veiled, and it was probably really awful. But the one thing that it had, that I knew something about, was racism. The knowledge of racism of that eighteen-year-old boy was very sophisticated because of direct experience. The rest was just crap.

When I was a child, we went on a family hike on ponies, an expedition to a high glacier in the Himalayas. It involved staying the night in a government rest house, then going to the glacier and coming back. So you would spend two nights in the guest house then come back to the city. Somehow, the pony that was supposed to be carrying the food wasn't. So we got to this government rest house, and there was no food. There was me and my sisters and my mother—who was extremely worried. We sent emissaries into the village, and they came back saying, "No, there's no food." And we thought, *It's a village! What do you mean there's no food?* They said, "No, there's no food."

About half an hour later, we saw a small procession coming from the village bearing food and apologies, because they had thought we were Hindu. When we were Hindu, there was no food. The moment we were a Muslim family, the food showed up, and they were apologetic. I was maybe twelve years old, and that was my first direct experience of sectarianism. Bombay on the whole, in the '50s and '60s, had virtually no Hindu-Muslim trouble. People were proud that this was a town in which that kind of strife didn't happen. Now, sadly, Bombay has become quite sectarian, but then it was quite a shock to experience that.

ZANGANEH: Is it true that the landscapes of Kashmir, the way you saw them as a child, left a strong mark on your imagination?

RUSHDIE: Kashmir is spectacular. You have these huge mountains around this tiny valley. It recurs in my work over and over. First, it's the beginning of *Midnight's Children*, then a fantasy version is the setting for *Haroun and the Sea of Stories*, and *Shalimar the Clown* takes on the subject directly.

ZANGANEH: You also talk about the fact that you were a nerd, that you were very lonely when you were in boarding school with few other *Lord of the Rings* fans there.

RUSHDIE: Yes, I was a *Lord of the Rings* nerd, that's for sure. I had a history teacher who gave me a copy; I almost failed my end-of-term exam because I was lost in Middle Earth. I can't do it anymore, but there were periods when I could recite some of the Elvish, and even the words engraved on the inside of the One Ring, which are in the language of Mordor.

ZANGANEH: Did you read a lot when you were a kid?

RUSHDIE: I've always been a bookworm. I think a lot of writers begin as readers. The only exception I've ever heard to this is V.S. Naipaul. I was at the Hay Literary Festival in the UK, and Naipaul was being interviewed, like this, in front of an audience. The moderator asked which books had influenced him, and what did he like and admire, and he drew himself up rather wonderfully and said, "I'm not a reader. I'm a writer." I thought,

Wow, that's so impressive! To have the courage to say that. But that was also the time when he was saying that he was better than all women writers who had ever lived. All of them. Better than George Eliot, better than Jane Austen, better than everybody. When he was asked why he was so sure of this, he said, "Women's writing is weak because they are not masters in their own house." You can imagine how well that went down.

Other than Naipaul, most writers I know are big readers. Growing up in Bombay, reading the books of England and America was my first knowledge, really.

ZANGANEH: You read Conrad?

RUSHDIE: I didn't read Conrad. I'm not like you! You're the one who read *The Satanic Verses* when you were fourteen! Not all of us do that. I was reading children's books because you know what? I was a child.

I remember reading this series of children's books by a writer called Arthur Ransome, which were known collectively as "Swallows and Amazons," because there were these two families who had boats, and one of the boats was called "Swallow" and one of the boats was called "Amazon." It was two families of children in the Lake District, sort of sailing on the lake. I remember being very impressed by how much personal freedom these children had. Their parents let them go off in these boats unsupervised, and sleep on islands by themselves. I thought this was real fantasy. How could children possibly be allowed to behave like this? It made me think that England must be an amazing place, because you could run wild. In fact it isn't, and you can't. But the books were great.

It's very interesting which books travel. For instance, *Alice in Wonderland* I read as a child. But *Winnie-the-Pooh*? It somehow didn't get there. I read the Winnie-the-Pooh stories much later, when I was too old for them. Some wonderful American books didn't get to India at all, like *The Phantom Tollbooth*. I had to discover that, again, much later.

ZANGANEH: The first time I ever saw you in real life was in 1999 at a reading at Harvard, when you'd just published *The Ground Beneath Her Feet*. I was so surprised, because most writers are not very good speakers, and you read so eloquently. At times it seemed that you were looking at the audience, and I was wondering if you were actually talking or reading.

Then you mentioned that you'd wanted to be an actor, and all of a sudden it made sense.

RUSHDIE: I discovered quite early that it was probably not a great idea, but when I was at university, I spent much more of my time involved in student theater than, say, involved in student journalism. I did write a little bit for the student newspaper, *Varsity*. And there was this little student magazine at the time called *Granta*—I seem to remember I did a couple of cartoons for them. Then it went bankrupt, it disappeared. It was this old student magazine that I drove into bankruptcy. Many years later, at the very end of the '70s, early '80s, it became revived, or the title was available. Bill Buford was able to buy the title for a hundred pounds or something, and revive it as a literary magazine. *Granta* is interesting because it has a very effective second act. It's again a very significant magazine.

ZANGANEH: You dedicated *The Enchantress of Florence* to Bill Buford.

RUSHDIE: Bill's period of editing *Granta*, which was through the '80s, made it a house magazine for a lot of us who were emerging writers at that time. People like Martin Amis, Ian McEwan, Julian Barnes, Kazuo Ishiguro, Angela Carter, Jeanette Winterson, Ben Okri... It was quite a remarkable moment in British literature, and *Granta* became the magazine where we would all give stuff. So my relationship with Bill was very close. Then he published *Haroun and the Sea of Stories*, and did a wonderful job.

One of my great disappointments is that we did a beautiful illustrated version of *Haroun and the Sea of Stories*, which the American publisher declined to publish. So the English edition of it, which is now out of print, was incredibly beautiful, but it was never published here.

ZANGANEH: Yeah, there are no drawings in my book.

We were talking the other day about Nabokov. He talks about having left Russia, and how much it influenced his writing. Of course, he's a writer of nostalgia. I think much of his obsession with adolescence is an obsession with Russia and with first love. What was the first rift with India, with your childhood?

RUSHDIE: I've always been, for obvious reasons, very drawn to writers who cross language frontiers; Nabokov is one of very few writers who were great in more than one language. Brodsky, yes, Brodsky's criticism in English is great, but his poetry not so much. Beckett I suppose, but the list is very small.

ZANGANEH: And Conrad is a fake one.

RUSHDIE: Conrad is different, because yes, he wrote in English, but he never wrote in Polish. He wrote in a language which wasn't his mother tongue. I was always interested in that: What happens when you leave not just the place, but also the language?

For me, it's a little bit different, because growing up, I spoke English, too. I went to what is called an English-medium school, where English was the medium of instruction.

ZANGANEH: What did you speak with your parents?

RUSHDIE: Urdu, mostly. My mother spoke very good English, but she didn't like speaking it. She said—a wonderful phrase—she said it made her tongue feel tired.

ZANGANEH: I understand that, actually.

RUSHDIE: They both spoke excellent English, but the mother tongue tended to be what we spoke at home. At school, it was English. So I grew up bilingual, with bits of these other languages, too: bits of Gujarati and Marathi, which I haven't really retained. My Urdu declined to the point at which I would write letters home and my mother would tell me how bad my Urdu was.

In the end, language chooses you. By the time I began to think about being a writer, there was no choice of language. There was only one language I could have been a writer in. And English has become an extraordinary vehicle for the world to express itself. I think it has something to do with the syntactical flexibility of the English language. You can do anything to it. You can twist it and turn it and tie it in knots, and it still works. Which, for example, French, not so much. French is a more classicist, more syntactically controlled language, which doesn't allow play to the same degree that English does.

Let's start right here. In America, English has gone through so many metamorphoses. There's not just one English here, there's a whole range of them. The English of the South is not the English of the North, the English of African Americans is not the English of WASPs, and so on. English has shown itself to be capable of reflecting the realities of many different kinds of experience. Of course, the Irish did this quite early on. Part of Joyce's language project was to create an English which didn't belong to the English. Then there's Caribbean English. Poets like Walcott and so on have made a West Indian English, and there are African and Australian variations of English...

I started out trying to do something of that sort with Indian English, because I felt that the very classical English of, let's say, the E.M. Forster tradition, didn't sound like the noise I heard in the streets. The question was how to make an English that sounded like that noise. I thought, *How do I manage to create the sound, the effect, of that polyglot speech in a book that's largely written in one language?*

I did feel that if I had been in India trying to write *Midnight's Children*, it would have been impossible. It's an amazingly megalomaniac idea, that you can somehow contain the whole of India in a novel. It's insane. When you're in India, it's obviously insane, because you realize you can't contain even one street in a novel, let alone hundreds of millions of people. When I was at school in Bombay, the figure we were taught for India's population was 450 million. That was, let's say, exactly sixty years ago. 450 million. And now it's 1.3 billion.

The further problem that arises is the place isn't there to go back to. When people say, "You can't go home again," that doesn't mean that you can't get on a plane. Of course I could go back, but *it's* not there, because *it's* not the same. The Bombay that I grew up in doesn't exist in the same way anymore. Remnants of it exist, but it isn't there anymore.

But I'm actually not by nature nostalgic. I'm much more interested in the moment I'm living in, what is happening around me now, and what do I think about that.

ZANGANEH: Hence *Fury*, and hence your last novel.

RUSHDIE: Yeah, the novels have moved over here, really. I want to read a little bit from *The Ground Beneath Her Feet*, because *The Ground Beneath Her Feet* was my first book that was largely set here. But it's set in the New York of the '70s, a very different place. Here's a bit about the business of distance:

In every generation there are a few souls, call them lucky or cursed, who are simply *born not belonging*, who come into the world semi-detached, if you like, without strong affiliation to family or location or nation or race; that there may even be millions, billions of such souls, as many non-belongers as belongers, perhaps; that, in sum, the phenomenon may be as "natural" a manifestation of human nature as its opposite, but one that has been mostly frustrated, throughout human history, by lack of opportunity. And not only that: for those who value stability, who fear transience, uncertainty, change, have erected a powerful system of stigmas and taboos against rootlessness, that disruptive, anti-social force, so that we mostly conform, we pretend to be motivated by loyalties and solidarities we do not really feel, we hide our secret identities beneath the false skins of those identities which bear the belongers' seal of approval. But the truth leaks out in our dreams; alone in our beds (because we are all alone at night, even if we do not sleep by ourselves), we soar, we fly, we flee. And in the waking dreams our societies permit, in our myths, our arts, our songs, we celebrate the non-belongers, the different ones, the outlaws, the freaks. What we forbid ourselves we pay good money to watch, in a playhouse or movie theatre, or to read about between the secret covers of a book. Our libraries, our palaces of entertainment tell the truth. The tramp, the assassin, the rebel, the thief, the mutant, the outcast, the delinquent, the devil, the sinner, the traveler, the gangster, the runner, the mask: If we did not recognize in them our least-fulfilled needs, we would not invent them over and over again, in every place, in every language, in every time.

No sooner did we have ships than we rushed to the sea, sailing across oceans in paper boats. No sooner did we have cars than we hit the road. No sooner did we have airplanes than we zoomed to the furthest corners of the globe. Now we yearn for the moon's dark side, the rocky plains of Mars, the rings of Saturn, the interstellar deeps. We send mechanical photographers into orbit, or on one-way journeys to the stars, and we weep at the wonders they transmit; we are humbled by the mighty images of far-off galaxies standing like cloud pillars in the sky, and we give names to alien rocks, as if they were our pets. We hunger for warp space, for the outlying rim of time. And this is the species that kids itself it likes to stay at home, to bind itself with—what are they called again?—*ties.*

AUDIENCE: Considering your affinity for film, what directed you into writing novels? How did your experience writing the screenplay for *Midnight's Children* differ from writing a novel?

RUSHDIE: A movie is a completely collaborative act. You do it with someone else: The director Deepa Mehta and I worked very closely together. A screenplay is only a step on the way to the work, not a work in itself. I remember Deepa was so respectful of me that when she was on location shooting the film and something wasn't working, she would call me. The time difference from Sri Lanka to New York is sort of insane, so we were talking to each other at very weird times of day and night. She was saying, "I want to remove this line," and eventually I said, "Deepa, stop calling me. You're there making the film; if the line doesn't work, cut the damn line. Stop calling me at 3:30 A.M.!" Because we had a good relationship we were able to trust each other in that way.

I enjoyed the collaborative process of *Midnight's Children* because it's the opposite of what I do for a living, but I like the idea that I sit quietly by myself and I make something, and when I've finished making it, it's made. I don't rely on actors to interpret it, or photographers to photograph it. If it's bad, it's my fault, and if it's good, nobody else gets to take the credit.

AUDIENCE: In *Haroun and the Sea of Stories*, a running theme is that they have neglected the old stories. Considering that your recent book *Two Years Eight Months and Twenty-Eight Nights* is actually based on *The Arabian Nights*, do you still feel that we neglect old stories too much?

RUSHDIE: I'm a great admirer of old stories. Folklore, fairytale, and mythology all over the world contain a lot of the collective wisdom of the human race. You go and visit it, and it's always a rich experience. *The Ground Beneath Her Feet* is in part inspired by the myth of Orpheus and Eurydice. If you want to tell the story of Orpheus and Eurydice, you can do it in fifty words or less. It's a paragraph. Yet there's an unbelievably concentrated amount of information about love and art and death compressed into this extraordinarily small space. You can start unpacking it, and it becomes like Mary Poppins's bag: An endless amount of stuff comes out. I think mythology is that kind of magic bag, that you can just go on and on and on unpacking it.

Storytelling is a great human pleasure and need. You don't have to be a professional writer; we all do it. When children are born, once children feel that they're safe and loved and fed, the next thing they want is a story. "Tell me a story." That desire for story is deep in the DNA: We are the storytelling animal. We are the only creature on this Earth that does this very strange thing of telling itself stories to understand what kind of creature it is. Some of those stories are true stories, some of them are made-up stories, some of them are family stories, some of them are national stories, some of them are religious stories, but we all tell ourselves these stories, and through those stories we understand ourselves. We are a narrative animal.

This conversation took place at the 2016 PEN World Voices Festival.

GARDENER'S MEMORY

Catherine LaFleur

We were gardeners of easily tamed plants,
with names that sounded vaguely erotic.
Dancers. Big Boy, Luscious Leaf, Climax.
Our hearts hungered like the belly. At night
my teeth dreamt of sinking into ripe flesh.

We grew gardens of easily tamed plants.
Tomatoes marshalling in orderly rows
firing over the heads of tender kneeling
lettuce, beans twirling sinuously up poles.
Every plant obedient to the garden rules
until the year of melons.

We built containers for easily tamed plants,
but cantaloupe, watermelon, honeydew with
viney runner legs and stretchy arms are
distance sprinters, who quick casual shed
the confines of the tiny fence and demand to
live at liberty in the yards of our neighbors.

Standing at the back fence of this small prison
staring into the outside, I sprinkle dried
seeds of cantaloupe, watermelon, honeydew
stolen out of the prison trash. Hoping not to be
easily tamed. One day I will grow far
enough away and free of this concrete steel garden.

Catherine LaFleur won first place in poetry in PEN America's 2016 Prison Writing Contest.

A LIVE DOG BEING BETTER
THAN A DEAD LION

Brigit Pegeen Kelly

Rain. Rain from Baltimore. The ballroom floor
Is lit. See the gold sheen on the over-
Whelmed grasses? See the starched ruff of the hedgerow?
And the dancers are dressing. They tease
Their toes into shoes. Tease their breath into stays:
Stay the moment. Stay the luck. Stay, stay, the fields
Are full of rain and baby's breath. These will
Fashion the heart, and the heart fastened to the sleeve
Will break fire as the redbird did this morning
Bursting his small buttons against the glass. The glass
Was not black-hearted. It was an innocent pretender.
It took to itself the idea of sky and the bird bought
It, played his brave swan dive into our palms.
So let us wear it. Let us wear the bird like
A boutonniere to remind us that caution snares
Nothing. O the cautious are caught in the net
Of their cares: *Stop, No Turn, Leave Your Shoes*
At the Door. Please Don't Spit on the Statue and
Tokens Go Here. But the bird rode his cheer up.
Rode the high wire of his cheer up. Left
Without counting the cost his spittle-bright snail
Trail for the rain to erase, for the wind to wash
Out. Booted his small body beyond the Beyond.
Now the wrecked grace of the morning trails
Its tattered clouds. But they are flowers.
The pink flowers of Maryland turn softly above us.

From *USING LIFE*

Ahmed Naji

TRANSLATED BY BEN KOERBER

I met Lady Spoon outside the restaurant. She had on a long white dress showing her arms and a bit of cleavage.

"You smell really nice," she said, kissing me on both cheeks.

"It's Moud's cologne."

It was her neck that made me fall for her. She's nine years older than I am, but she knows how to stay youthful, exercising regularly and always eating healthy. She's pretty, cheerful, and has a successful career in advertising. Unfortunately for her, she's a Protestant and happens to love Egypt, and her chances of meeting someone with both these qualities in Cairo are slim at best. She studied overseas before spending quite a long time being terrified of getting married or settling down. Sometimes she'd like to have children. She had been used to dating men who were older than her, but suddenly they had stopped showing an interest. Those who did show interest didn't interest her. This was the first time that she would be dating someone younger than her, which made her embarrassed to tell her friends.

The name "Lady Spoon" was given to her by Mona May. She saw her once at a concert wearing a pair of spoon-shaped earrings.

These were the same earrings she had on now. They swayed with the movement of her hand as she chopped a loaf of bread. In spite of the dryness in my throat, I'd been smoking since I woke up this morning. Cigarettes have a different sort of taste with the morning breeze in Zamalek: something resembling bliss, desire, a softness in violet and orange.

Our breakfast was eggs, along with slices of the finest quality pork, imported from abroad. After honey, jam, and a glass of orange juice, I was back to life. As the poet says, "You ain't you when you're hungry." At Maison Thomas, her smile nudged me awake within a white bed.

We walked around the streets of Zamalek in the direction of her apartment. She had a thin silver bracelet around her ankle and toenails painted red. Sometimes we would walk hand in hand, and sometimes with my arm around her waist. Under the shade of the trees, we laughed. We shot smiles at the officers standing guard outside different embassies, but their solemn demeanor didn't change.

I thought…do I love her?

Of course I love her. I can't touch a woman I don't love. But then, what is love exactly? It's a relaxing of the heart, a tranquility in your soul, a warmth in your stomach. It's like any love in Cairo, always ready to disappear. A lover of companionship.

In her apartment, we smoked a joint of hash. I rubbed her knee as she played around on her computer looking for an old Madonna song. I lifted her dress above her knees and slid to the floor. Nestling between her legs, I lifted up her foot and started licking her big toe. I walked my tongue in gentle taps along her leg until I reached her knee, which I pummeled with kisses.

"It tickles," she giggled in English.

I gave her knee a parting kiss, and continued my tongue's journey up her thigh. I planted a kiss, soft as a butterfly, on her thinly-lined underwear and pulled it away with my hands. I plunged my tongue into her pussy. I drank a lot that afternoon. I drank until I felt thirsty. I gave her a full ride with my tongue before she took me into her room, where we had slow and leisurely sex. She turned over, and I put my fingers in her mouth. Wet with her saliva, I stuck them in her pussy. Slipping and sliding. I stuck them in from behind. I grabbed her short hair and pulled it toward me. I humped her violently and then lay on top of her for a few seconds. I got out of bed and threw the condom into the trash. As I gave her a smile, the phone rang.

"Hey dude, where you at?"

"Mona…what's up? I'm in Zamalek."

"So, you still up for a beer tonight?"

"Maybe…"

"I'm with Samira. We're going up to Muqattam Mountain."

"So you've got a car?"

"Yeah."

"Okay then. Why don't you come pick me up in Zamalek?"

"When?"

Lady Spoon climbed out of bed with a gentle smile. Sex was over now. We've still got some friendship and goodwill on our faces. People are eating each other alive out there, so why can't we keep things civil?

Ahmed Naji was the winner of the 2016 PEN/Barbey Freedom to Write Award.

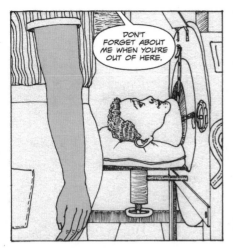

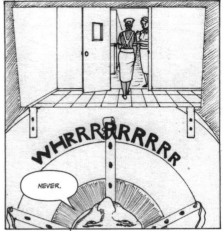

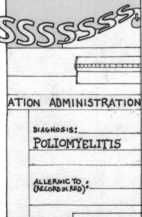

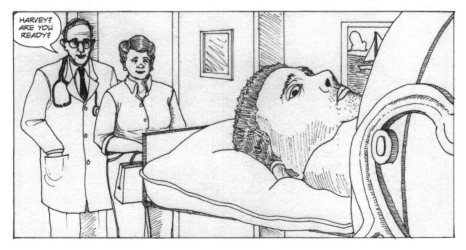

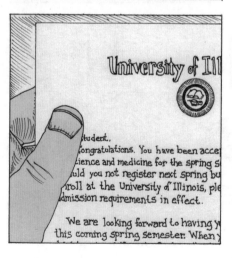

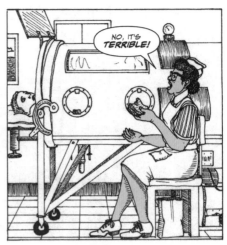

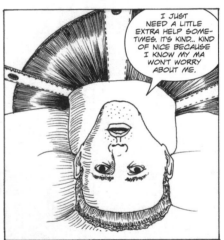

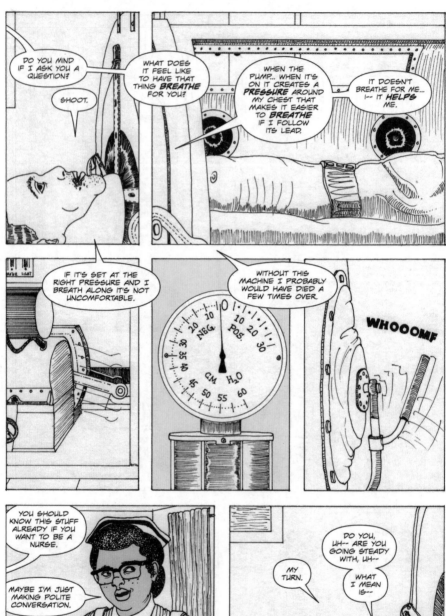

MATTIE!

I'D BETTER GO.

YES, NURSE FIELDS?

THERE ARE **MANY** ROOMS IN THIS HOSPITAL.

WE ONLY ALLOW YOU WITH THE POLIO PATIENTS BECAUSE WE'RE SHORT-HANDED AND THEY REQUIRE SO MUCH ASSISTANCE.

WHAT ARE YOU--?

YOU HAVE SUCH AN AMBITIOUS FUTURE PLANNED FOR YOURSELF. THINK ABOUT WHAT WOULD BE **APPROPRIATE.** DO YOU UNDERSTAND?

YES, MA'AM.

...WHOOOMF... ...WHOOOMF... ...WHOOOMF!...

THAT OLD NURSE IS SUCH A BITCH...

I WONDER WHAT THEY'RE SAYING.

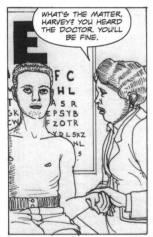

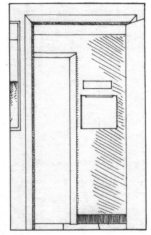

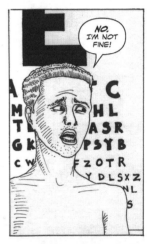

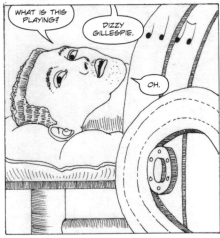

© Josh Trullio

BECOMING THE CHAPLAIN

Ben Kingsley

Adderall flicks a light switch on inside your head. Meth is the Sun. My brother told me that once. He tells me nothing now while he sleeps on a glorified gurney. The slinky organ of his ventilator struggles up a fogged tube and back down. He has always been sickly. Sometimes self-inflicted. Sometimes by Quetzalcoatl the soul-ferrying snake god, he would say through a smile. This time everyone was to blame. Gods and men. Meth had sucked the calcium from his body. A starburst of baldness on the back of his head. A nailless naked toe edging past sheets. We found him this time—well, I found him this time—on his hands and knees on a sewer grate just outside the city. He was dragging a garbage bag full of clothes. I assume to sell. He sure as hell wasn't wearing anything six other people hadn't lived half their lives in.

What we doin' 'bout your brother here? When the doctor placed her hand on my shoulder she didn't bother to take the nibbled Bic out from between her fingers.

I bend over him to ask if he remembers when I was eleven and he was eight and I was still in Scouts. When he was staying home fragile in a racecar bed and I wanted to fight him wanted to kill him for all the paltry things. But couldn't do more than bring him packed pudding. Does he remember that overdrawn Indian summer when everything we would become together hovered just above our heads? When they made me the chaplain and Matthew DiBrito patrol leader and he called us the Trailer Boys until I finally got out to high school. Does he remember the twins and our now-married neighbor Nutcase Casey? The other week I dreamt I was back at camp dropping a stone into a lake of remembering. I hummed my brother lots of things. Things that whimpered on the edge between waking and forgetting. Things that still hover just above our heads even now:

There was a panting of flesh. I ventured closer to the edge of the creek.

The deer.

I thought he was a felled log, so enormous yet emaciated grey and speckled with life. He lay on his side and I saw a width of branching antlers scrape stone. Labored breaths. Bats veered in the dark and crickets called to one another and watched beside my boots as I stepped out of them. I undid my uniform and left it balled at my feet. I stood at the edge. My bare feet met the slush of river and the stream sipped me in. When I reached him, would he talk to me? The voice of an old god in my hands. I waded toward him and he was still. His stone altar was warm against my wet body and when I crawled to his side I could feel the thrum of heart that hung within. His eyes were bright from blood loss. Like giant drops of pitch. Breathe in and. Wine-dark spittle flung from his nubs of teeth. Breathe out and. Insects hovered and lighted around his head. They roosted on his stained coat. They nested between his shovel-shaped shoulders. Electric ticks plied to his heaving. Even partly submerged in the river, he was taller than me. We faded alongside each other.

Blue light loped out of the night's black hide and on my knees I took his horns in my hands. I thought about things that whimpered on the edge. War and pain and white hospitals. Marbles of blood swam from his thighs like dimpled red fish being birthed into the river and I pressed his head under. He tensed and kicked crippled hooves further into the silt and marl. Little life splashed around us. Illuminated. Still he was unable to lift himself from the hammered face of rock.

Close to the water I sounded an oath in an unfamiliar tongue and I stuttered over every word.

On my honor I will do my best to do my duty to myself and my country. To obey the Law. To help other people and other creatures at all times. To keep myself awake.

I pushed him farther down.

A scout is loyal. A scout is kind. A scout is brave and a friend.

My little breath sputtered against the river. His coat prickled against my chest. The river seethed and his brown head was a blur. I felt deeper creatures I could not see in the darkening waters.

A scout is reverent.

He was still and clouds fled the fresh-lit sky like painted sprites.

————

After I am old and bent from time and all materials the deer will be re-born as some great warrior or so I hope. And so I hope a man I love will likewise be divided back into his origins. I lie again small and young next to my brother, we two small-bodied specks amid a great swell of living afterbirth. His eyes like giant drops of pitch. I feel the beat of his fading heart against my breast.

What we doin' 'bout your brother here? When the doctor placed her hand on my shoulder I didn't bother to tell her about the deer and the river or what it meant to be the chaplain. My brother slumped there be-neath the sheets, enormous, emaciated, grey.

MR. LEVI

Jeremy Mulligan

My first day on the job was uncomfortable. I felt like a question mark at the beginning of a sentence, out of place and hard to read. As discreet as the staff tried to be, the racial overtones were evident. Thanks to them, I learned that when Caucasians joke about something, it's usually a way of expressing their true feelings or intentions, softening the blow so to speak. I was introduced as Remy to some, and Mr. Mulligan to others. Their mouths said *Hi how are you*, but their facial expressions spoke louder. Exclamation point, question mark, period, period, comma. I was a black prisoner from Detroit working in the infirmary/medical department of a prison situated on the outskirts of West Virginia. The only black suit at the wedding.

On my third day of training, outside one of the cells, Pete said to me, "That's Mr. Levi. I go in there and bust it up with him from time to time to keep his spirits up. He's dying..."

"Dang... from what?" I asked. I looked inside the cell and saw a black man who seemed to be in his early sixties, at the oldest. He sat up in a hospital bed covered in a blanket from the stomach down, wearing glasses over a pair of bright eyes. I sized him up and didn't notice death anywhere. "He's got stomach cancer," Pete answered after following my eyes.

Not much time passed before I felt like a project or challenge to the staff. How long could I ignore their humor, their racist or homophobic wisecracks? I noticed the staff cut their eyes at me after every joke to evaluate my response. Searching for a chuckle, a forced smile, anything that would signal the okay for them to joke with me. Tension grew as I ignored them. I was left out, perceived as uptight, walking into rooms that all of a sudden got silent. I can't recall the exact date, but I'll never forget the feeling I got the first time I smirked at their humor. It felt like I was chipping away at a part of me, awkward, like knowingly stepping in the wrong direction.

The first time I walked into Mr. Levi's cell, the air was stale, a musky scent lingered, and his eyes seemed distant. Maybe death was near. I greeted him with *whatsup man* and smiled. He nodded and gave me that look black men give each other when we're outnumbered. A quick search for camaraderie and assurance, the cornerstone being steady eye contact.

The ice was broken by this silent pact: We talked and he never spoke of death. He spoke of life, the foods he used to eat and the dishes he wanted to try. We reminisced, laughed, argued, and repeated the cycle over the course of a week. I shaded the bubbles on his commissary sheet for him while trying to influence him to eat healthier. He held firm, an old man stuck in his ways. The fire was reignited in both of us, and Mr. Levi gave my job meaning.

Mr. Levi's condition limited him to an ice-cream-and-resource diet; he despised this. I sat under corrections officers who complained when he asked for his ice cream on time. They prayed for his downfall. Cancer had recruited some teammates, and I wanted Mr. Levi to know it. Their logic was, the more difficult his stay, the sooner cancer would win its fight. The staff declared war for purposes unknown, as if a deathbed wasn't enough.

To them, I was the basketball star Dwyane Wade's twin; I also resembled Chris Tucker and a few other brown-skinned celebrities. The joke was that we all look alike. I fed into this conversation unconsciously. I began to justify laughing at their jokes in order to keep it cordial, but underneath, it felt like I'd lost a layer. My spirit took a major blow. That evening, Mr. Levi and I discussed race and media stereotypes in contrast with our current surroundings. As our conversation ended, he told me to be careful, as if his intuition gave him X-ray vision.

Mr. Levi's pride wouldn't let him beg for ice cream. If he was asleep when meals were served, or couldn't get it down at the time, the ice cream wasn't stored; it was thrown away or offered to us. He increased his snack consumption from the commissary even though it was bad for him, and he even ordered a flat screen TV.

"It's my money," he countered after my Hispanic co-worker and I questioned the purchase. For a second, I think we forgot his confinement. A cell, hospital bed, wheelchair, and the inability to control his bowels or shower on his own. With that said, a plasma TV and ice cream wasn't an extravagant bucket list.

Maybe I'd tolerated one too many jokes that day or suppressed too many thoughts. It was at a point where the best of me and worst of me were trying to figure out, *Who's this new me?* That's how it feels when you begin to slip against the grain, defying your inner core. This particular day, Mr. Levi needed "assistance." Usually that meant talking and spending time with him, so I held up my index finger. But the corrections officer found time for him before I did. How had it come to this?

Mr. Levi needed help penning and addressing a letter. I grabbed the notepad and sighed irritably while the CO sat back and enjoyed. It was only three sentences, but I treated it like Mr. Levi wanted me to write his autobiography, impatient, disregarding his feelings. I read over his legal document aloud, and as he tried to elaborate I snapped, "Look man, I don't need to know all that, just let me know what else you need me to do!"

"Forget it," he snapped back but his eyes said something different. They were filled with anger and hurt. Chuckles floated in the background from the CO, who saw signs of victory. I think Mr. Levi saw death for the first time that evening—not in himself, but in me, in the spiritual form.

"They say he denied the treatment," my co-worker confided to me after Mr. Levi slept through two of our shifts. "But I think they just told me that to be safe so I won't say nothing because they don't wanna treat him and they really want him to die."

My brain raced. Why would he order a brand new TV, accept weekly visits from family, then all of a sudden refuse treatment?

Our final encounter is on continuous playback in my head. Days went by and he still wasn't awake. The staff peeked in on him like an exhibit, offering comments like, "Yup, he's still breathing," or "That old fucker ain't dead yet?" I observed from afar with other motives, hoping to get a shot at redemption. If only I could catch him awake to erase our last memory. I worked overtime to no avail. I witnessed his eyes do cart-wheels, blinking with only the whites visible. His body slumped and his breathing slowed.

The irony plagues me: Perhaps he decided to let go at the same time I did, after our last encounter, when I let go spiritually. Mr. Levi's final look at me adds weight to this belief. He passed on three days after we clashed, and I watched him cry before I watched him die.

Mr. Levi chose to go, but the question remains: Did I choose, too?

Jeremy Mulligan won an honorable mention for essay in the 2016 PEN Prison Writing Contest.

PHOENIX

MJ McGinn

It was my job to kill rats. To tie rats inside a metal and leather machine that held them tight, still. To stick a cigarette in their knife-point rat mouths. To light it. To wash blood from my lab coat. To calculate if smoke could kill them. To measure how long it might take. To write it all down.

Have you ever seen a rat smoke a cigarette? It's as bizarre as a painting of bulldogs in bowler hats playing poker.

I must have watched a thousand rats die a thousand quiet deaths, watched their tiny, pink lungs devoured by ash and phlegm. Watched the white lab walls turn a sour yellow.

Once, I pulled Rat 3, group D, from his cage, his little legs flopped sideways, his body as limp as a wet, boiled hot dog. I put Rat 3, group D, on the gunmetal table and pumped his chest with my pointer finger to the beat of "Stayin' Alive" by the Bee Gees.

Alive again, he squirmed between my fingers like a minnow.

I am all silence now. The ghost rats are the only ones listening. They're waiting for me, smiling, salivating, cigarettes between their jab saw teeth, measuring the life of a man.

THE SHOOTINGS

Hubert Mingarelli

Translated by Sam Taylor

Kropp was touchy. Not a bad guy, but a bit of a loner and very sensitive. After the first killings, he had said, "I'm not doing that." He'd left the clearing where they were taking place, he'd gone back toward the trucks, and he'd said, "Give me something else to do. I'll bring food. I'll bring drink. I'll clean trucks, whatever you want. I don't care. But I'm not doing that."

Everyone got their hands dirty that day. Nearly all of us suffered. But not him. So everyone cursed him. He took the brunt of the company's hatred and contempt. Some wanted to beat the shit out of him. It nearly happened. Graaf wanted to kill him. And he would have done. But the commander intervened. "Who will pay for this?" Kropp asked him. The commander didn't answer, but he was an understanding, accommodating man, and he arranged for Kropp to be sent to the kitchen to replace the real cook, who had jaundice. That saved Kropp's bacon, and he remained the cook. And after that, people had to stop cursing him, of course, because he was the one filling our mugs and our plates. Because it was up to him how much broth and salami and bread we got.

We asked to see the commander. What else could we do? We were able to go over Graaf's head because he'd left to see an acquaintance in town—thankfully, as I doubt he'd have let us do it otherwise. The commander looked away as he listened to us, his hands fidgeting in his pockets as though he were searching for something. We didn't hold back when we spoke to him. He was a bit older than us. In civilian life, he bought and sold fabric in bulk. It was difficult for us to imagine that, though, because for us he had always been some sort of commander.

We weren't telling him anything he didn't already know. Occasionally he would glance toward the door, or give quick little nods. Not because he was in a rush, but because he understood us. We exaggerated a little bit, of course. Here, if you wanted an inch, you always had to ask for a mile. If the cook were to start being a bit stingy with his portions, for example, we would have to say that we were starving to death, otherwise nothing would ever change.

That evening, what we had to say was more important, and our commander understood this. We explained to him that we would rather do the hunting than the shootings. We told him we didn't like the shootings: that doing it made us feel bad at the time and gave us bad dreams at night. When we woke in the morning, we felt down as soon as we started thinking about it, and if it went on like this, soon we wouldn't be able to stand it at all—and if it ended up making us ill, we'd be no use to anybody. We would not have spoken like that, so openly and frankly, to another commander. He was a reservist like we were, and he slept on a camp bed too. But the killings had aged him more than they had us. He'd lost weight and sometimes he looked so distraught that we feared he would fall ill before we did and that another, less understanding commander would be appointed in his place: someone we didn't know, or—worse, perhaps—someone we did know. Because it could easily be Graaf, our lieutenant. *He* didn't sleep on a camp bed. He took good care of himself, but not of us. With him in charge, there would be less coal and more marching. With Graaf, we would be ceaselessly filing in and out of the base. When we thought about this, we could hear the iron echoing from dawn till dusk. It went without saying that we liked our commander, no matter how distraught he was.

As usual, he gave us what we asked for, and we left the next morning—Emmerich, Bauer, and me. We went at dawn, before the first shootings. That meant missing breakfast, but it also meant not having to face Graaf, who would be filled with hatred that we had gone over his head. It was still dark, and everything was frozen. The road was harder than stone. We walked for a long time without stopping—in the cold air, under the frozen sky—but we weren't unhappy, in spite of that.

And it was as though I'd lied to the commander the previous evening, because that night, for once, I didn't dream about our life here. I dreamed that Emmerich, Bauer, and I took a tram together. It was a perfectly simple dream, but extraordinary for that very reason. The three of us were sitting, and around us all was peaceful and—in contrast with most dreams—entirely realistic. There was nothing to suggest it was false, that the scene existed only in my mind.

I didn't tell Emmerich and Bauer about my dream. I worried that they would start telling me about theirs. Here, good dream or bad dream, the same rule applied: better to keep it to yourself. In fact, why keep it at all, even for yourself?

THE LAST STAND

L.P. Sutton

I was walking through the parking lot on the way to my husband's office, past half a dozen hearses, when I thought again about torching the place. It used to be a professional building. There was an optometrist and a pharmacist, a chiropractor, two physical therapists. There was even an acupuncturist for a while when new age medicine made its way to the suburbs via Oprah.

But for a year or more, it had been nothing but the goddamn funeral home and Paul's little dental operation. The corridor outside his office had pew-like benches and flower arrangements in whites and pastels. During services, portraits of the dead on plywood easels framed the entrances. The smell of carnations made me gag.

Paul still had his two rooms—a reception area where no one ever waited and the examination space with separate nooks for mixing plasters or developing X-ray film. He'd inherited all his equipment when he bought the practice thirty years ago. The instruments looked heavy, but pretty much everything still worked. When I suggested updating, he'd shake his head and tell me air compressors hadn't changed in a hundred years. I didn't believe him, but you don't make a marriage work by saying everything you mean.

As the other professionals went, so did Paul's business. New patients didn't want to contemplate casket options while getting their root canals. Paul's old patients dropped off too. Not all at once. Some moved out of the area, others lost their insurance. A woman he had known since her teens was killed in a car accident. Her husband, who had also been Paul's patient for years, took her to the funeral home next door. We had to go to the service. I had one black dress left that almost zipped closed. I wore a cardigan over it; no one had looked at me in years. On the lapel of his suit jacket, Paul wore a pin from his dental fraternity.

I tried not to think of any of these things as I clipped on my bib and leaned back in Paul's exam chair. He made a slow show of reviewing my chart and then laying out peroxide gel and the laser. I'd been in four times over the last six weeks, for bleaching treatments we both knew I didn't need. My teeth had been sensitive to begin with, and now I could barely handle a cold drink or even the brisk air on a morning walk. All my nerves were on end. But Paul wanted to complete the treatment, and it was easier to go in. He had become quick to argue about everything, and his face had taken on the look of someone in permanent disbelief—eyes fixed wide, brows raised—as if the gradual deterioration of his practice still required his indignation. I knew it for what it was—an old man's Alamo—but I couldn't tell him that.

So I let him bleach my teeth and hoped they wouldn't fall out of my head. Paul leaned in for a closer look. "There's still noticeable discoloration on the lower incisors," he said, like he was quoting my progress for a medical textbook. His soft belly pressed into my side. Our weight was one more thing I had been meaning to fix about us. But I'd already seen three kids through from birth to adulthood, and I was tired.

I counted the perforations in the acoustic ceiling tiles and hoped Paul would hurry. He loomed over me as he worked, giving me a direct view of his nose hair and the blackheads clogging the pores around his nostrils. I closed my eyes.

"I work and you nap," he said, and I heard the beep signaling him to move the laser over the next segment of my teeth. "Figures."

I couldn't speak. My jaw was fixed wide by a plastic vise. But I opened my eyes and blinked rapidly to show my disagreement, and then I made myself keep my eyes open for the rest of the session. I wouldn't give him the satisfaction.

When he was finally finished, he penciled in a return appointment.

"My teeth have never been whiter," I said.

"I'm not finished." He handed me a little reminder card with my appointment date and time.

I turned the card over in my hands. All the other doctors I saw—my internist, my gynecologist, my optometrist, even my dermatologist—sent me appointment reminders by email. I clicked once on the email and the appointment added itself to my calendar. Paul didn't even have a computer in the office. "If you weren't working," I said, in my sweetest voice, the one I used on my most dejected students, "think of all the trips we could take." I'd been encouraging him to retire ever since the chiropractor left the building. He was the only other tenant to hold out against the funeral home's expansion half as long as Paul.

"That's something to look forward to," Paul said, but he snapped my chart closed. "Foot fungus from hotel bathrooms. Coach airfare where they herd you in, starve you, and gamble on the slim chance you won't get a blood clot. Elbowing Japanese tourists for a snapshot of a fucking church that looked better in a twenty-five-cent postcard."

If I'd had any energy left, I'd have turned on my heel and walked out on him. Instead, I reached for his hand and tried again, hating myself as I did it. "We've got some savings, Paul."

He pulled his hand back. "I'll see you at home," he said, and stashed my chart in the bookcases he used instead of file cabinets.

When the eviction notice arrived, I was relieved. Paul came home from the office as I was browning ground beef for a lasagna and pulled the letter from his pocket. The landlord was giving him six months and would chip in on his relocation costs.

"It could have been worse," I said. I thought the offer was generous. Paul's lease had expired years before, and the funeral home had more than once tried to buy him out. The landlord could have turned him out with just a few weeks' notice.

But thirty years in the same office had made Paul territorial. "Are you an idiot or a moron?" he said. He pinched a mouthful of beef from the pan, then spit it out into the sink. I'd been cooking for him since our third date, when he'd spent half the night praising my rack of lamb. "I pay rent, I have rights. I'm getting a lawyer."

Paying a lawyer meant no money for traveling or for redoing the kitchen. I was about to argue, but Paul didn't give me the chance. He stomped off and left through the garage.

I wasn't surprised. He had reacted badly even at the earliest signs of pressure from the funeral home, when he might have gained a little leeway by being friendly and accommodating. The funeral home had first complained that the noise of his air compressor disrupted their mourners, and instead of looking into a newer, quieter model, or the cost of relocating the thing to the other side of his office away from the chapel, Paul bellyached to the landlord. It didn't occur to him that his landlord would naturally be aligned with the other, bigger tenant.

Paul was back sooner than I would have liked, with a greasy paper sack. Apart from his belly, the new weight showed mostly in his face. His jaw had birthed a second chin. But his arms were still ropey with muscle, and his back broad and solid, a safe harbor where I liked to rest my head. Part of me wanted to start over, lean into his big strong back and do whatever it took to reverse the direction we were heading in. I suggested we open a bottle of wine. I had the lasagna in the oven already and for a split second imagined we could still salvage dinner. But he dumped out a pair of hamburgers from the sack and started eating without me.

I circled behind instead of joining him at the table. It was easier to talk when I didn't have to look at him. "You were planning to retire in the next few years." I tried to sound upbeat, flush with an enthusiasm I didn't feel. "Maybe this is a blessing, a real chance to do something else."

He shoved half a hamburger into his mouth, and I watched the back of his head bob as he chewed. "Everybody's rushing me," he said, and then he balled up the sack and threw it across the room toward the sink. It landed on the countertop a few feet away and bounced to the floor.

That night, I checked our savings online while Paul watched TV in the den. I'd only planned on teaching for another year or two. I'd get a small pension after that and keep the district's health insurance for us both. It didn't seem like enough though, to live off just my salary or pension when we'd grown used to having two. And the added expense of a lawyer made it seem impossible. I didn't want to be stretching out coloring appointments between haircuts or washing my car myself or waiting for movies to come to cable. I'd done those things in my twenties and thirties, when we were first starting out and making a family. Since the kids had grown and gotten jobs of their own, Paul and I had lived without a budget. I couldn't imagine going backward.

I waited until Paul left for work the next morning before going to see the only real estate attorney I knew. He was our neighbor down the block, retired now but still sharp, and I figured I wouldn't get a bill for knocking on his front door. I had phoned my principal and faked car trouble to buy myself an hour or two.

Harry seemed surprised to see me. I tried to remember the last time I'd been to his house. It had to have been three or four years before, when his wife was still alive. She'd been diagnosed with breast cancer that spread to her bones. I apologized for barging in on him.

"It's not like I have a train to catch," Harry said and stood aside to let me in. He was only a few years older than me but looked ancient, his shoulders rounded, the hair on his beard and eyebrows an almost translucent white. I followed him to the kitchen where he pointed me to a chair at a small oak table. "Joann was the cook. I don't do much more in here than press Start on the microwave. But I can put up coffee. Would you like a cup?"

I could have kicked myself for not bringing over a pie or a banana bread. Joann and I had not been friends per se, but we had been friendly enough, and the thought of this man nuking meatloaf alone in his family's house, where three of the four bedrooms were empty now, made me feel awful. I thought of how Paul might handle years without me, and I patted Harry's big dry hand and accepted the coffee, though I wasn't sure I had the stomach for it.

"I've got cookies here somewhere, too," he said and buried his head in the pantry.

The house was neat but looked preserved, a museum of outdated curtains and tiled counters. There were photos of Joann and their children on nearly every available surface. Harry caught me staring at a row of snapshots from ski trips and weddings and graduations.

"We used to head up to Big Bear two or three times a year," he said. "The kids loved it."

"Great skiing up there," I said, and worked my face into what I hoped was a friendly smile. "But our kids always went for the summer sports. Surfing, beach volleyball, even Frisbee sometimes." Their kids had always been better athletes than ours. They had been better students too, and were probably working better jobs now and living better lives with better families. Neither Harry nor Joann ever said these things, but I felt them, year after year when their kids came home decorated with medals and trophies. No one could say ours were total failures—there were no drugs or teen pregnancies, and all three of them made it through college—but they were hesitant in the world somehow and clung to routine. I would have traded a bit of trouble to see a real fire in any of them. Though I tried not to show my disappointment with them, it was hard not to feel like Paul and I had missed something, done some fundamental thing wrong to shortchange them.

Harry shuffled to the table with two mugs of coffee and a box of shortbread tucked into his armpit. "I don't think you came here to talk about skiing or surfing."

I explained what was happening with Paul's practice. Harry said "okay" a few times but never interrupted. Though I knew I was saying too much, it felt good to tell someone. Until the words were coming out of my mouth, I hadn't realized how much the whole thing had gotten to me. When I finished, Harry asked if Paul had looked for another office space.

"He doesn't have enough patients left to make that work." I felt like a traitor. My ears burned. But I had to get it all out. "Plus, there's his pride."

Harry sighed and turned the coffee mug back and forth in his hand. A beat passed. "Understood," he said finally.

I stood up. "I shouldn't have bothered you."

He reached for my wrist and said, "Maybe we could buy him a little more time. Would that be enough?"

"It might," I said and sat back down. I couldn't imagine it being enough, but I was willing to consider almost anything. Paul had never liked dentistry. His mother had insisted that all her children be professionals. She told Paul he could be a doctor, dentist, or lawyer, and she'd pay for it. He chose the easiest of the three. Or at least that's how he liked to tell it years later. I think he was secretly relieved. Like our children, he didn't seem to have a passion for anything in particular, and his mother had freed him from responsibility for his own choices. He could build his life around being a good provider and then blame his mother when that didn't feel like enough. I wondered what our own children blamed on me.

Harry pushed the shortbread toward me and explained that Paul could send his landlord a check for the full year's rent. If the landlord cashed it, it'd be a good argument for a year's lease, and any landlord would have a hard time resisting that kind of money up front. "Your husband could leave feeling like it was on his own terms."

"He needs that," I said, and chewed on my lip to keep from crying. I couldn't remember the last time I'd cried in front of someone else, and I didn't want to start then. But neither saving the practice nor ending it felt right.

Harry looked uncomfortable and shifted in his chair. "Most of us do."

The thing no one tells you about teaching is how much of it is just you. Your personality and temperament on full display. In graduate school, our instructors whined about pedagogical strategies, institutional models for dealing with particular types of students given particular resources. It took me about ten doe-eyed minutes in front of my first set of rowdy fifth graders to understand that pedagogy didn't help. I found out right then and there what kind of person I was, a person who had a dozen creative ways for saying no but not one of them discouraging. As a result, the students in my classroom were more focused and attentive than most, and I'd received handfuls of county and state teaching awards.

Paul went to every awards ceremony with me. He congratulated me for each bit of praise I received, no matter how trivial it seemed. I knew I was just an elementary school teacher, not a rocket scientist or cancer curer or worldly executive, but Paul's recognition—even more than my students' or their parents'—made me feel like I was living a full, maybe even an important, life.

For a long time, I'd tried to give a little of that feeling back to him. But he liked dentistry even less as the years wore on, and my cheerleading wasn't enough to counter the forty hours a week of self-loathing at the office, or those painful social occasions where mingling began and ended with the question he hated most: So what do you do? He got a dog from the pound and took to walking it practically into the next county each night after dinner. When that dog grew old and died, he got another. I had joked at first that he was married to our dog, but then he really *was* spending more time with the dog than me and it wasn't funny. I'd catch him rubbing the dog's ear under the table and my blood would boil. When the last dog died and Paul wanted to adopt another, I put my foot down. By that time, he was preoccupied with the funeral home and didn't fight me on it.

All that day in my classroom, I mulled over Harry's idea. I didn't love it. It might not work and it meant putting up almost our entire bank account. We had a bit more money socked away in a separate investment account, but that was for our retirement and most of it wasn't liquid. Still, I shared the idea with Paul that evening after work. It was the only possibility I had to offer.

Paul was quiet at first and then surprised me by going straight for the drawer where we kept our checkbook. I had expected another argument, and yet there he was scribbling down a number big enough to buy us each a new car. He was calmer, more resolute than I'd seen him in months. He wanted to run the check to the landlord right then and there.

"Can it wait until the morning?" I had broiled a pair of steaks and they were resting on the counter, the potatoes were cooked through.

"Ever since you got fat," he said, and though his voice was level, a vein bulged in his neck, "you think dinner is the most important thing in the world." He took a few steps toward the garage, then turned back to add, "The world doesn't stop because you want dinner, Ellie."

I opened my mouth to say something but the air hit my bleached teeth and made me want to jump out of my skin. Paul slammed the door behind him and then I heard him start his car and leave. I stood there dumb for a minute, maybe longer. The man I'd married had never been soft-spoken, but he'd been reasonably careful with me. I had no idea where that man was. I tipped the steaks from the cutting board into the trash and then sat in front of the TV. A sitcom played but was nothing but noise and colors swirling before me. At some point I gave up on watching and went back for the steaks, which I rinsed under the faucet, and even the potatoes.

I had started in on the second steak when my daughter called. I put the phone on speaker and listened to maybe every other three words she said. It wasn't anything she hadn't told me before. She was upset again about the long East Coast winter. The year before, I had tried to talk her out of the move, but she was sure that she and her husband would adapt. Their pipes had burst twice because the old house they thought of as quaint wasn't well-insulated and the two of them didn't have the sense to leave the tap open. As she rattled off the expense of the repair, I knew she was hinting for a handout, so I steered the conversation back toward me, where she'd lose interest quickly. "I saw my internist last week," I said. It wasn't true but it was plausible.

"What's wrong?"

"Not a thing. Clean bill of health." That also wasn't true. I knew that if I had actually seen my internist, I'd have a laundry list of chronic conditions to address, starting with high cholesterol, high blood pressure, and arthritis in my hands.

"That's great, Mom," she said and I knew she had stopped listening. In the background, her husband called to her. "So you and Dad are doing fine," she said mechanically, like she did when she would call weekly from college. She would take thirty seconds to go through the motions of asking about us before she launched into a half-hour recap of what she had been doing.

"I'm fine," I said, though my chest felt heavy and hollow at the same time. I took another bite of steak. "If you want to know how your father is, ask him."

"Great," she said, and hurried off the phone.

When Paul came home, the TV was still on. My empty plate with the two rib bones and the two foil wrappers from the potatoes sat on the coffee table like an indictment. He was carrying another one of his fast food sacks, the grease stains already soaking through the paper, and he sat on the opposite end of the couch.

We'd been together too long to bother with the silent treatment. I asked him if the landlord took the check.

Paul didn't look at me. He had tipped the contents of the sack onto the coffee table and was spreading out his French fries. "After hours," he said, and squirted ketchup over the fries. "I left it in his mail slot." Red beads of ketchup splattered the table. I waited for him to wipe them up. He didn't. He shoved the fries into his mouth two or three at a time, and the splatter spread from the table to the carpet.

I got up for a bottle of stain remover and started to spray everywhere. Paul hunched protectively over his food and shouted, but I kept spraying. The mist of chemicals grew heavy, a cloud poised over the coffee table. I whispered, "How do you like that burger now?" as I walked out of the room.

In the morning, I drove to the bank before work and told the first teller I saw that I needed to stop a check. I handed over the card for our joint account, watched the teller type a few keys, and it was a thing done. I should have felt guilty or ashamed, but I did not. The weight on me, all those months of not acting on what I wanted, gone as soon as the teller pressed Enter. But less than twenty-four hours later, Paul had spotted the fee on our account for the stopped check. As I was getting dressed for work the next morning, I heard him shouting on the phone in the den at the bank's customer service department. "You've botched this. I don't know how, but you've botched this."

I crept into the den. I had pants and a bra on but hadn't decided on a blouse yet, and it had been a long time since I'd been even half naked in front of him. He was slapping the checkbook against his thigh as he yelled. I reached behind him to take the phone. As he grabbed for it, I pushed a button to end the call and felt the same rush of energy that had come over me at the bank. Something felt possible again. I didn't know what, but for the moment, I'd take it.

He looked at my finger on the button and then all over me. I squared my bare shoulders and sucked in my gut, and I waited for the tirade, for the torrent of insults. I gripped the phone at my side. I had been truly afraid of him only one other time, when he found one of his mutts dead in our backyard where I had laid down poison for the rats nesting in the rose bushes.

His eyes lingered on the roll around my middle before they lifted and found mine. His jaw was slack, his face soft and raw. I took a step toward him, but he let the checkbook fall to the floor and walked out of the den, leaving me there with the dead phone in my hand.

THE SETTING SUN

Nate McKowen

My dad was homeless. We still spent the weekends together every now and then. We called it "camping." "Your dad's here," my mom called when his van pulled into the driveway.

I tossed my phone on the counter, arms extended, as if to say, *See what deprivation I must endure.* I didn't get service on the other side of the mountain. No doubt there would be a thousand missed texts when I got back. She would be all drunk at 2:30 and want me to sneak over to her house. I would be camping.

I climbed in and tossed my sleeping bag in the back. I thought about how lucky other kids with divorced parents were. They could say they were going to their dad's house for the weekend. I couldn't say that. I was going to where my dad "lived." His house rolled with him—chipped, dented, and gunmetal grey.

"Hey, bud," he said, shifting the Oven into drive. Dad appeared almost as defiant as he was. A mountain-man beard and long hair framed a face wrinkled by countless hours in the Arizona sun. His skin was cured cowhide. As he drove, his crooked fingers, armored in calluses, bent around the steering wheel, and his shoulders hunched forward from a car accident that had crushed his spine when he was younger—or maybe he was weighed down by a lifetime of disappointment.

"Hey," I said back.

The ride out to the Valley was quiet. We sat in silence, listening to the rattle of the engine, engaged in a mental tug-of-war, judging how the other felt and imagining what sort of walls had been erected between us over the past few weeks. At the freeway exit that led to the Tucson Mountains, we passed a derelict waterpark. I liked to imagine that normal families had spent weekends there, dads doling out bills so the kids could get ice cream, applying liberal amounts of sunscreen, the children laughing like they do on commercials. Then everyone would pile in the SUV for a comfortable ride home in the AC, content that life was as it should be. But I could never really know. The waterpark was a scar on the side of I-10, and the green waterslide that cut through the trees stood like a broken monument to what it was not.

Picture Rocks was about forty-five minutes outside the city. We headed west over the Tucson Mountains, and since we always went in the afternoon, the sun blinded us as we rolled over the crest of the mountain. The Saguaro National Monument spread out before us, bathed in dying light, untouched and unspoiled. My heart always lifted at this moment, like the strings of expectations had been cut and all my pressures released—although more likely it was because the van was going downhill.

This part of the trip never failed to make me feel like I was in a Western movie. We were two cowboys riding into the setting sun, leaving the world behind.

Maybe this is what men do, I thought. They don't talk about how they feel. They keep their faces passive, their demeanor taciturn. Words are cheap. Life is too complex.

Manly or not, I didn't like the silence.

After the quiet snuggled itself between us, I said, "When the water rises, so, too, does the boat."

"What's that?" he said, distracted.

"From *The Book of Five Rings.* Some famous samurai wrote it."

The corner of his mouth pulled up, and I knew what he was thinking. Me and my Eastern philosophies were a point of humor with him. He thought it was just a phase I was going through. Even if he was right—because I had found all the same faults in those religions as I had in his—he didn't need to know that.

Religious debate was frequently our main form of conversation. He was raised Roman Catholic; I didn't know what I believed in. When I was five, my dad told me that Santa Claus wasn't real; I wanted to return the favor. My position had three points. One: I told him it was hard for me to swallow the story that God had spoken to a few guys and told them to write down what he said. To me, that sounded like schizophrenia. Two: Men were fallible creatures, and if they wrote a book, it was for their own agenda. Three: For millennia, the Catholic Church had used that same book to further their own ends, saying it was "in God's name." In my adolescent arrogance, my argument was flawless. He usually agreed with what I said. However, that never shook his faith. He was too stubborn to admit defeat. He said that for thirty years these arguments had kept him from God. That had all changed the night those three guys attacked him.

At the time, he was camping out under a tree just across the street from the Wagon Wheel. Most everyone knew he was out there, including the cops, but they didn't bother him because he kept to himself and didn't cause any trouble.

One night, three drunk idiots stumbled into his camp. He woke just in time to see the blade of a shovel slam down on the crown of his head. Lights out. When he came to, he told me, he just planned to lie there and bleed out, slip into oblivion, that the peace would be nice. They took everything he had, which wasn't much. He did what most men do once or twice in life: He asked God for a sign. Then he decided that he wasn't going to give up yet. He hauled himself up and staggered across the street. They took him to the hospital. Even though he didn't have insurance, the doctors stitched him up and told him he was lucky to be alive. The cops came and asked him if he knew the guys who did it. He said no, and even if he had, he wasn't the type to point fingers. A few days later a little girl at the community center handed him a Bible, told him to keep it. To hear him tell it, he never saw that girl again.

We pulled into the place we were going to make camp for the night, a little patch of desert far away from everything. He started a fire. I dragged two boulders to each side of the pit and we set a rusted grill on top. We ate London broil that night. The musty scent of creosote filled the air. Above, the night sky disrobed and showed us the secret that she saves only for those who venture outside the city. The stars were brighter than I could ever remember.

"That's what capitalism does," my dad said. "For someone to win, someone has to lose."

Even though I wasn't much of an economist, I liked these discussions. I sat with my back straight. Just two men talking about the state of affairs.

"Yup." I nodded my head in agreement.

"It's like a country club," he continued. "You're either one of the boys, or you're everyone else."

We let the obvious hang between us. My dad used to play golf at a country club when he was my age. My grandfather had been a member, owned an insurance company, had a license to fly a private plane. I had learned this from other family members because my dad never talked about his father. I only knew that my dad hated country clubs.

When the steak became pieces of gristle on the grill, I asked him a question that I had never voiced aloud. "Why do you live like this, Dad?"

He considered it a moment. "Money's tight."

"So get a job."

"Any job I know how to do would leave me crippled in a week." He fidgeted a bit. "You know, you sound like them."

"Then get disability," I told him.

"I'm not disabled."

"Neither are half the people on it."

He looked me in the eye. "I'm not a liar, either."

Neither was I: I told him how I really felt. "What kind of footsteps are you putting down for me to follow in?"

He got quiet. I regretted saying it immediately.

His voice came in a whisper. "I've always been honest with you. Never tried to pull the wool over your eyes. I'm sorry you don't like the way I live, but this is how life turned out. This is me. This is God's plan for me, apparently."

That made me mad. "That's bullshit. Don't hide behind God. If you wanted to, you could get a job bagging groceries or something."

He snorted. "Bust my ass for two hundred bucks a week? I wouldn't be able to get an oil change with that. I make more money selling metal."

"You sell wrought-iron javelina on the side of the road. That's not a job. That's like a gypsy or something."

He looked at me hard. A smile cracked through. He laughed. I couldn't help but laugh too.

Nate McKowen won third place in memoir in the 2016 PEN Prison Writing Contest.

PATRICK STEWART

Fortunato Salazar

Alone in the double-wide, I'm listening to the clothes dryer repeat the word "replica" over and over, I'm in a replica trance, I don't hear my phone when it buzzes. I'm tranced out and meanwhile the actress is leaving a message on my voicemail—but the actress is so good that at first the message freaks me out. I've been ransacking the CVS bags, mine and hers.

The message isn't anything special. "Hello Nietzsche, this is God." It's all in the delivery.

Meanwhile the stray is barking at the back door, not the stray's usual nuisance exhibition of vocal stamina, but a clear message, DEFCON *woof*, insisting that I release the stray. And outside the door are peacocks. I don't have to open the door to be sure that peacocks are lurking in the yard, trained peacocks, geared-up peacocks, reconnoitering the yard, tied to a feed, or worse.

The last time the stray barked like this was the middle of the night. I quieted the stray and listened carefully and heard nothing. I opened the front door and there at my feet was a bloody stain. Blood, fragments of bone and feathers, very tiny fragments. I instructed the actress to stay in bed. I brought the stray back to bed and described the bloody stain. The actress, in the voice of Patrick Stewart, intoned a verse, "Nature red in tooth and claw." Which was exactly the phrase running through my head...and to hear what was running through my head, spoken by Patrick Stewart while the actress moved her lips, freaked me out, too, but not as much as the sheep.

The way the actress leaves the message, it sounds like she has the Stormtrooper helmet on. I actually *can't prevent myself* from going into the laundry room. But of course the Stormtrooper helmet is right there, along with the golf club and the baseball bat.

The sheep: The tinbender lives up the gravel road, his peacocks in a tin shed when they're not reconnoitering. Up beyond the tinbender there's the stray that resembles a white wolf and limps out of the brush to beg for scraps. Up beyond the curve in the road are the llamas. But as far as I know there are no sheep for miles around.

Eventually I'll have to open the door because not to open the door will be an admission that my jitters are getting the better of me.

So I open the door, but first I put on the Stormtrooper helmet. I hoist the stray up into my arms, the black and white stray, the white Stormtrooper helmet. A fuck you to anyone who's at a remote monitor and watching, waiting for my jitters to get the better of me, so that I don't storm out onto the back deck, confront the peacocks.

Jitters, but realistic jitters. Because the tinbender *is* a tinbender. And Leland was always saying, "The tinbender, now there's someone who learned his craft." Plus, in this neighborhood, you would not expect drones. You might expect a suspicious tinbender to wire cameras onto harnesses and fit peacocks with the harnesses. So that when a peacock wanders down the road, hops the fence into your yard, turns toward you and makes its display, you're being watched. The eye of the peacock is the tinbender's eye.

The actress had the tinbender down pat, same with Leland. She would do a whole routine of Leland and the tinbender, jawboning about hunting safety. Safe hunting practices and the role of obesity and the insidious fatigue that creeps in at the end of the day. Leland and the tinbender—no obesity there. I was gaunt from all that plundering of the CVS bags, and then there was the actress, who had always been gaunt.

I open the door and naturally the stray already knows, the stray has heard. Immediately a vicious struggle begins in my arms, Stormtrooper versus stray, an apocalyptic struggle, it would be fun to watch, the powerful and compact stray writhing violently, just at the limits of containment within the Stormtrooper's wiry arms, on the verge of bursting out, tearing deep scratches in the Stormtrooper's unhealthy pale skin.

I'm beginning to understand that this struggle is the first stage of an epic clash between two armies. The army of the tinbender, peacocks wired with harnesses that carry incendiary devices; the army of the stray, the stray who was bred to seek out and eviscerate. The stray, senses on high alert; the peacocks transmitting surveillance imagery to the tinbender.

And I understand now that I've been wrong about the sheep. The sheep aren't the beginning but *a* beginning. In their wraithlike clanging across the yard, which only the stray can hear, the sheep dragging their chains aren't supposed to be the ghost of Leland, a first ominous visitation—not a visitation but a prophetic message of the coming epic clash.

I've been dipping hard into the CVS bags and now I'm sweating inside the Stormtrooper helmet, even though the clouds are low and gray and cold beads of mist have welled up on the sealed surface of the deck.

And I see clearly that what I must do is announce the prophetic message. Go back into the double-wide, through the hall into the bedroom, the actress on the mattress on the floor. Tower over the mattress with the stray still writhing in my arms; I'm the herald of the epic clash, the chosen Stormtrooper, reporting. I can already feel my larynx striving to force the message down two octaves, so that the message, waiting ages to be spoken, will resonate inside the helmet, build in force, before emerging from the frown in the helmet, ringing, oracular.

Fuck. It's slipped my mind that the actress must be in New Mexico by now.

But it doesn't matter, the epic clash is on. The message has begun to form inside the helmet. Not exactly apocalyptic, but the peacock won't be standing there forever, brandishing its fanned tail. "You're meddling with powers you can't possibly comprehend."

MASTER FILM

Solmaz Sharif

my mother around that blue porcelain,
my mother nannying around the boxed grits and just-add-water pantry
of the third richest family in Alabama,
my mother at school on Presbyterian dime and me
on my great grandmother's lap singing
her home, my mother mostly gone
and elsewhere and wondering
about my dad, my baba, driving a cab
in Poughkeepsie, lifting lumber in Rochester, thirtysomething
and pages of albums killed,
entire rows of classrooms
disappeared, my baba downing Bud Light by the Hudson
and listening to "Fast Car," my baba on VHS
interviewed by a friend in New York, his hair
black as mine is now, I'm four and in Alabama, I see him
between odd jobs in different states,
and on the video our friend shows baba a picture
of me and asks *how do you feel when you see Solmaz?*
and baba saying *turn the camera off* then
turn the camera off and then
can you please look away I don't want you to see my baba cry

A COVERED UP PAST

Tsering Woeser

My father took more than three hundred photos documenting the Cultural Revolution in Tibet; one of these photos is truly shocking. It shows a raging flame continuously unfolding, burning thousands of pages into ash. Among them were many years-old Buddhist scriptures. From the picture it is not clear who lit the fire and who was just standing around watching, but their faces all look excited. Images showing people dressed the same way, with the same facial expressions, appeared from many other areas across China during the Cultural Revolution, but the Tibetan-style buildings in the background remind us: This is Tibet, this is Lhasa, this is the Sungcho Rawa of Jokhang Temple, the special place to recite Buddhist scriptures.

What could be stolen was stolen, what could be smashed was smashed, what could be burnt was burnt. But there were simply too many books to steal, smash, or burn. So they were thrown onto the streets or into the toilets. My mother remembered: "Once, I went to visit Uncle Tsering to deliver some things. It was the first time that I left home after giving birth to you. From the Yabzhi Langdun home, at the military area backdoor to the Lubu Bus Station, from the east of the Barkhor all the way to the surveillance station, the streets were full of books, I didn't know where from, from nearby temple halls that were destroyed or monasteries that they were stolen from. They were all Buddhist texts, and there were many of them, more than autumn leaves; walking on them made a crunching sound. I was a little scared, felt that stepping onto Buddhist scriptures was a crime. But I could not help it, there were simply too many and no way to avoid them. I felt uncomfortable, wondered why people would even dare to walk on Buddhist scriptures, let alone crush them; they were all dirty and broken. It was in the fall, the book pages together with leaves were blown into the air by gusts of wind. This scenery left a deep and long-lasting impression on me."

My father's cousin who now lives in Kathmandu told me in a still fearful voice: "The broken Buddhist statues were put into backpacks and emptied onto the streets; the pages of Buddhist scriptures were torn out and scattered onto the road. I was frightened. Every time a statue was smashed, every time I stepped onto a scripture page, this feeling came up. But there was nothing I could do. They even used engraved wooden manuscript covers as toilet lids. Kunchok Sum! People would defecate and urinate on them. What a crime! They had these toilets at Meru Temple and Ramoche Temple; another one was installed in the neighborhood committee of Meru Temple. People were afraid to use these toilets, but if they didn't, local officials would shout at them."

Many elderly Buddhists felt sorrowful when seeing all the important objects being destroyed, quietly wondering what the point was in living this long. By getting this old, they had even witnessed the death of the Bodhisattva; is there anything worse than that? When I was young my nanny, Acha Yeshe, shook her head and said: "It is really true. Even the Bodhisattva was killed during the Cultural Revolution."

ZOFRAN

Dilruba Ahmed

Then, the atrophy of appetite.
We brought your favorite stew:
potatoes, the forbidden beef. We brought
coffee with sugar and cream. Surely,
the smell of it, the steam…
You would not. So we scalded
our tongues with food meant
for you. We found the coconut sweets
you liked but you would not. The insult
of their stripes: pink, brown, white—
a flag from a country to which
you couldn't return. We slipped
the candied cubes from the wrappers
meant to keep them fresh,
innocent and useless.

A covered dish arrived—*Don't open it.*
Another tray arrived—*Don't. Open.*
Meal after meal that you would not eat.
You could not.
The sea in you refused to cease movement.
Even the doctor's amber pills
you heaved aside like so much beach glass.
Outside each leaf began to bleed yellow
like dampened saffron
as we yielded one grief to the next.

THE STICK

Nicole Callihan

At the mouth of the cave was a stick.
These are the things I did with the stick:
chewed it, waved it to the sky, poked myself
in the eye, pretended it was a daisy, pretended
it was an orchid, a tulip, lily, cigarette,
made it into a gun and shot my brother,
nudged my brother to make sure he was dead,
nudged my brother to make sure he wasn't dead,
licked it like a lollipop, sang into it like a microphone,
brushed my hair with it, brushed my tongue,
gagged myself with it, gagged myself again,
made myself throw up, made myself cry,
made myself look pretty, made myself
sit in the car alone, made myself practice
writing my first name with the last name
of a boy I loved, whipped my knuckles with it,
my thighs, dug little stars into my forearm,
tried to beat off a man, tried to beat him harder,
tried to use it as a megaphone, tried to pry
my mouth open and say the words out loud,
made it into a Calculus equation, an airplane,
a gun again, pointed it to the sky,
prayed over it, moved to Brooklyn with it,
took it to the bar, punished it, ignored it,
pretended it wasn't mine, put it in the corner
of that dirty little apartment on 12th Street,
let the cat piss on it, wrote bad poems about it,
slept with it, let it touch me in places I had never

been touched, let it scratch the very itch it made,
took it to a candlelit dinner, packed it up into a U-Haul,
turned it into an altar for my wedding,
danced with it instead of with my father,
took it on my honeymoon, didn't breathe a word of it
to my husband, shoved it to the back of the junk drawer
in our new home, forgot where I put it, searched for it,
found it only after I forgot I was looking,
let it accompany me to the hospital, bit on it
while the baby was being born, bit on it
while the next baby, the sick one, was being aborted,
bit on it when the littlest was born, tried to prod myself
awake—my God, I was tired, all those years of nursing,
of thermometers and backrubs and mommy,
mommy don't go—started sleeping with it
under my pillow, took it to therapy, gave it a name,
hid it behind my back when my husband walked in,
danced with it, wrote it an inappropriate email,
wished I had buried it by the mouth of the cave
when I still remembered where the cave was,
used it to call my mother to see if she remembered
the cave, turned it into a peace offering, until finally
I tied a string to it and dangled the string into the river.
There, after one thousand years, I caught a fish.
But the fish was too small, so I threw it back in.

CONTRIBUTORS

VIVIAN ABENSHUSHAN was born in Mexico City, where she studied language and literature at the National Autonomous University of Mexico. She has contributed to *Cuaderno Salmón*, *Letras Libres*, *Nouvelles de Mexique*, and more. Abenshushan won the Gilbert Owen Short Story Prize in Mexico in 2002, and was featured in the 2009 edition of *Best of Contemporary Mexican Fiction*.

DILRUBA AHMED's first book, *Dhaka Dust* (Graywolf Press, 2011), won the Bakeless Prize for Poetry awarded by the Bread Loaf Writers' Conference. A writer with roots in Pennsylvania, Ohio, and Bangladesh, Ahmed holds a BPhil in creative writing and an MAT from the University of Pittsburgh. She is a graduate of Warren Wilson College's MFA Program for Writers, and a lecturer in creative writing at Bryn Mawr College.

AYAD AKHTAR's plays include *Disgraced*, *The Who & The What*, *The Invisible Hand*, and *Junk*. He wrote the novel *American Dervish* and the screenplay for *The War Within*. Recent honors include a Pulitzer Prize for Drama, two OBIE Awards, the Outer Critics Circle John Gassner Award, and nominations for Independent Spirit, Tony, and *Evening Standard* Theatre awards.

BORIS AKUNIN's popular Erast Fandorin novels have sold more than eighteen million copies in Russia, as well as being translated into thirty languages. *Planet Water*, the penultimate title in the Fandorin series, was published in 2015 in Russia by Zakharov. Akunin won the Antibooker prize for *The Coronation*, and was named Russian Writer of the Year in 2000.

ROZINA ALI is on the editorial staff of *The New Yorker*. From 2013 to 2015, she was a senior editor at *The Cairo Review of Global Affairs* in Egypt, and continues to serves as one of their contributing editors. Ali's writing has appeared in such publications as *The Guardian*, *The New York Times*, *Al Jazeera America*, *Foreign Policy*, *Salon*, and *HuffPost Live*.

KWAME ANTHONY APPIAH is a British-born Ghanaian-American philosopher, cultural theorist, and novelist. His books include *Color Conscious: The Political Morality of Race*, and the novel *Avenging Angels*. Appiah was the Laurance S. Rockefeller University Professor of Philosophy at Princeton University before moving to New York University in 2014. He holds a joint appointment at NYU's Department of Philosophy and School of Law. Two collections of his lectures, *As If: Idealization and Ideals* and *Mistaken Identities*, are forthcoming in 2017.

ANITA AUGUSTIN was born in Klagenfurt, Austria. She studied philosophy and drama at the University of Vienna before embarking on a PhD. Augustin was awarded the Lise Meitner Literary Prize for her short story "number thirty-eight." She made her debut as a novelist with *Der Zwerg reinigt den Kittel (The Dwarf Cleans the Smock)*. Augustin's second novel, *Alles Amok (All Amok)*, was published in 2014.

AZIZA BARNES was born in Los Angeles and lives in Oxford, Mississippi. Her first chapbook, *me Aunt Jemima and the nailgun*, was the first winner of the Exploding Pinecone Prize and published by Button Poetry. Her first full-length collection, *i be, but i ain't*, was published by YesYes Books in 2016.

TOMMYE BLOUNT is the author of the poetry chapbook *What Are We Not For* (Bull City Press, 2016). A graduate of Warren Wilson College's MFA Program for Writers, Blount has been the recipient of fellowships and scholarships from Cave Canem and the Bread Loaf Writers' Conference. He lives in Detroit, Michigan.

NICOLE CALLIHAN's books include *SuperLoop* (Sock Monkey Press, 2014), and the chapbooks *A Study in Spring* (2015), *The Deeply Flawed Human* (2016), and *Downtown* (2017). Her poems have appeared in *PANK*,

Painted Bride Quarterly, and *The American Poetry Review,* and as a Poem-a-Day selection from the Academy of American Poets.

ANNE ENRIGHT is an Irish author and a Fellow of the Royal Society of Literature. She has published novels, short stories, essays, and one non-fiction book. Her novel *The Gathering* won the 2007 Man Booker Prize. She has also won the 1991 Rooney Prize for Irish Literature, the 2001 Encore Award, and the 2008 Irish Novel of the Year.

KEITH GESSEN is a founding editor of *n+1.*

FRANCINE J. HARRIS is the author of *play dead* and *allegiance,* a finalist for the 2013 Kate Tufts Discovery Award and the PEN Open Book Award. She was a 2015 National Endowment for the Arts fellow and a 2008 Cave Canem fellow, and is a writer in residence at Washington University in St. Louis.

HELEN HOFLING lives and writes in Brooklyn. She is a member of The Writer's Foundry MFA Program and co-chairs the poetry committee of the PEN Prison Writing Contest.

MARLON JAMES is a Jamaican writer. He has published three novels: *John Crow's Devil* (2005), *The Book of Night Women* (2009), and *A Brief History of Seven Killings* (2014), winner of the 2015 Man Booker Prize. Now living in Minneapolis, James teaches literature at Macalester College in St. Paul, Minnesota.

BRIGIT PEGEEN KELLY (1951–2016) was born in Palo Alto, California. Kelly received some of American poetry's most prestigious honors, including a Discovery/*The Nation* Award, the Yale Younger Poets Prize, a Whiting Award, and fellowships from the Guggenheim Foundation, the National Endowment for the Arts, and the Academy of American Poets.

JAMAICA KINCAID grew up in Antigua and lives in North Bennington, Vermont. Her novels and essays include *See Now Then, Mr. Potter, My Garden Book, My Brother, Autobiography of My Mother, A Small Place,* and *Annie John.* Among her many accolades are a Guggenheim Award for Fiction, a

Lannan Literary Award, and honors from both the American Academy of Arts and Letters and the American Academy of Arts and Sciences.

BEN KINGSLEY is best known for his Academy Award-winning role of Mahatma Gandhi. This Ben is a touch less famous. He is a VONA: Voices of our Nation Scholar and a Kundiman Fellow, and belongs to the Onondaga Nation of indigenous Americans in New York. His work has recently been published in *The Iowa Review*, *New American Writing*, *Pleiades*, *Prairie Schooner*, *PANK*, and *The Poetry Review*.

CATHERINE LaFLEUR is an incarcerated writer and a member of the Homestead Writers Collective. She plays the dulcimer and the piano. Her work has appeared in *Exchange for Change*, *The Voices Project*, and *Cream City Review*.

VALERIA LUISELLI is the author of the essay collection *Sidewalks* and the novel *Faces in the Crowd*, which won the *Los Angeles Times* Art Seidenbaum Award for First Fiction. Her most recent novel, *The Story of My Teeth*, was a finalist for the National Book Critics Circle Award and won the *Los Angeles Times* Book Prize for Best Fiction and the Premio Metropolis Azul at the Blue Metropolis Montreal International Literary Festival. Her books have been translated into more than twenty languages.

SARA MAJKA received graduate degrees from UMass Amherst and Bennington College and was awarded a fellowship at the Fine Arts Work Center in Provincetown. She now lives in Providence, Rhode Island, with her young son. *Cities I've Never Lived In* is her first book.

COLUM McCANN is the author of six novels and three collections of stories. He has received many international honors, including the National Book Award, the International IMPAC Dublin Literary Award, a Chevalier des Arts et des Lettres from the French government, election to the Irish arts academy Aosdána, the 2010 Best Foreign Novel of the Year Award in China, and an Oscar nomination. His work has been published in more than thirty-five languages.

MJ McGINN grew up in the suburbs of Philadelphia. He is an MFA candidate and teaches creative writing at Adelphi University. He received the 2016 Robert Muroff award for creative writing and the top prize in the 2011 55-Fiction writing contest.

NATE MCKOWEN graduated from the New York Film Academy. His passion is filmmaking, but during his sabbatical at the posh, state-sponsored gated community of A.D.O.C. (Alabama Department of Corrections), he discovered writing as a storytelling outlet.

RACHEL MCNICHOLL is a freelance translator and editor based in Ireland. She studied German, Italian, and French for her BA and German literature for her MA. Her work has been published in journals and anthologies such as *Mānoa*, *The Stinging Fly*, *No Man's Land*, and *Best European Fiction*. Her translation of a short story collection by Austrian writer Nadja Spiegel, *sometimes i lie and sometimes i don't*, was published in 2015 by Dalkey Archive Press.

HUBERT MINGARELLI was born in Mont-Saint-Martin in Lorraine. He won the Prix Medici in 2003 for his novel *Quatre soldats* (*Four Soldiers*). The English translation of his novel *Un repas en hiver* (*A Meal in Winter*) was nominated for the *Independent* Foreign Fiction Prize.

HAROON MOGHUL is the author of *How to Be a Muslim* (coming in June 2017). He writes for CNN, *The Washington Post*, and many more.

WALTER MOSLEY is the author of more than forty critically acclaimed books, including the bestselling mysteries featuring Easy Rawlins. His work has been translated into twenty-three languages and includes literary fiction, science fiction, political monographs, and a young adult novel. Mosley's short fiction has been widely published, and his nonfiction has appeared in publications such as *The New York Times Magazine* and *The Nation*. He is the winner of numerous awards, including an O. Henry Award, a Grammy, and PEN America's Lifetime Achievement Award.

GALA MUKOMOLOVA received her MFA from the Helen Zell Writers' Program of the University of Michigan. She is a winner of 92Y's 2016

Discovery/*Boston Review* Poetry Contest. Her poetry has been published in *Indiana Review, Muzzle, Nailed, Vinyl, The James Franco Review*, and *PANK*, among others. Monthly, she transforms into an astrologer called Galactic Rabbit. Lots of people believe in her.

JEREMY MULLIGAN is incarcerated at the State Correctional Institution at Greene in Waynesburg, Pennsylvania. He was awarded an honorable mention for essay in PEN America's 2016 Prison Writing Contest.

AHMED NAJI is an Egyptian novelist and journalist. He is the author of three books—*Rogers* (2007), *Seven Lessons Learned from Ahmed Makky* (2009), and *Using Life* (2014). He is a journalist for *Akhbar al-Adab*, a state-funded literary magazine, and frequently contributes to other newspapers and websites, including *Al-Modon* and *Al-Masry Al-Youm*. Naji has been a vocal critic of official corruption under the rule of Egypt's President Abdel Fattah al-Sisi, and was awarded the 2016 PEN/Barbey Freedom to Write Award.

GABRIEL OROZCO studied at the Escuela Nacional de Artes Plásticas between 1981 and 1984 and at the Circulo de Bellas Artes in Madrid between 1986 and 1987. Orozco gained his reputation in the early 1990s with his explorations of drawing, photography, sculpture, and installation. Avid world travelers, Orozco, his wife Maria Gutierrez, and their son Simón divide their time among Tokyo, Paris, New York, and Mexico City.

SUSAN OURIOU is an award-winning literary translator and fiction writer. She has won Canada's Governor General's Literary Award for Translation, been appointed a Chevalier in France's Ordre des Arts et des Lettres, and had translations on the IBBY (International Board on Books for Young People) and USBBY Honour Lists.

JEAN RHYS (1890–1979) was born in Dominica, and spent her childhood years there before moving to England at sixteen. Her novel *Wide Sargasso Sea* (1966), written as a prequel to Charlotte Brontë's *Jane Eyre*, won the WH Smith Literary Award in 1967. Rhys authored several novels and short story collections, as well as *Smile, Please* (Penguin Classics), an unfinished autobiography that was published posthumously.

SALMAN RUSHDIE's *Midnight's Children* won the Booker Prize in 1981, and was deemed to be "the best novel of all winners" on two separate occasions. He is the author of twelve novels, several works of nonfiction, and a collection of stories. Rushdie is a Distinguished Writer in Residence at New York University, and he was the founder of the PEN World Voices Festival.

FORTUNATO SALAZAR was born and raised in Mexico City and now lives in Los Angeles. His fiction and translation appear or are forthcoming in/at *Tin House, Mississippi Review, McSweeney's, Joyland, The Brooklyn Rail, The Los Angeles Review,* and elsewhere.

SAM SAX is the author of *Madness*, winner of The National Poetry Series (Penguin, 2017), and *Bury It* (Wesleyan University Press, 2018). He has received fellowships from the NEA, Lambda Literary, and The MacDowell Colony. He's the winner of the 2016 *Iowa Review* Award, with poems in *The American Poetry Review, Gulf Coast, Poetry,* and elsewhere.

SARAH V. SCHWEIG is the author of *Take Nothing with You* (University of Iowa Press, Kuhl House Poets, 2016). Her poems have also appeared in *BOMB, Boston Review, Literary Review, The Iowa Review, Tin House, The Volta,* and elsewhere. She lives in New York City with her husband and cats.

SOLMAZ SHARIF's writing has appeared in *The New Republic, Poetry, The Kenyon Review, jubilat, Gulf Coast, Boston Review, Witness,* and others. Her work has been recognized with an NEA fellowship, a Stegner Fellowship, and a Ruth Lilly and Dorothy Sargent Rosenberg Poetry Fellowship, to name a few. Sharif's first poetry collection, *LOOK* (Graywolf Press), was a finalist for the 2016 National Book Award.

TIMOTHY SMALL has served as the mentorship coordinator at the PEN Prison Writing Program since 2010. He teaches writing to undergraduate students at St. Joseph's College and helps coordinate the school's MFA program, The Writer's Foundry.

L. P. SUTTON earned her MFA at UC Irvine, and her JD from Boston University School of Law. She works as a divorce attorney in Los Angeles. Sutton's writing has been published in *The Rumpus, Faultline, The Georgia Review, Orange Coast Review, Blue Lake Review*, and too many court filings to count.

SAM TAYLOR is the translator of *HHhH* by Laurent Binet and the author of the novels *The Island at the End of the World, The Amnesiac*, and *The Republic of Trees*. He lives in France and the United States.

COLM TÓIBÍN is an Irish novelist, short story writer, essayist, playwright, journalist, critic, and poet. He is the author of eleven books, most recently the novel *Nora Webster* (Scribner). Tóibín is currently Irene and Sidney B. Silverman Professor of the Humanities at Columbia University, professor of creative writing at the University of Manchester, and chancellor of Liverpool University. In 2011, *The Observer* named him one of Britain's Top 300 Intellectuals.

JOSH TRUJILLO is a writer, editor, and comic book creator based in Los Angeles, California. He has worked with clients including Boom! Studios, Dark Horse Comics, Shanken Creative Group, and DC Comics, among others.

ARUN VENUGOPAL is a reporter on race, religion, and identity at WNYC, and recently worked on "The United States of Anxiety," named one of the best podcasts of 2016 by *The Atlantic*. His work has been featured in *The Guardian, The Wall Street Journal, Slate,* and *Salon*. He lives with his family in Queens.

ANTOINE VOLODINE is the heteronym of a French writer. He won the Grand Prix de l'Imaginaire in 1987. *Des anges mineurs* (*Minor Angels*), one of his best-known works, won the Prix du Livre Inter and the Prix Welper in 2000. He won the Prix Médicis in 2014 for his latest novel, *Terminus radieux* (*Radiant Terminus*).

GENE WALKER was born in Houston, Texas. He studied architecture at the Rhode Island School of Design, where architecture was discussed with enormous poetic emphasis. Walker was awarded first place for essay in PEN America's 2016 Prison Writing Contest.

ELIOT WEINBERGER is a writer, essayist, editor, and translator whose work has been published in more than thirty languages. Weinberger's many translations include *The Poems of Octavio Paz*, *In Light of India*, *Sunstone*, and Jorge Luis Borges' *Selected Nonfictions*, which received the National Book Critics' Circle Award for Criticism. His most recent collection, *The Ghosts of Birds* (New Directions), was published in 2016.

TSERING WOESER was born in Lhasa, Tibet Autonomous Region. Woeser is the author of numerous books, including *Tibet on Fire* (Verso Books), which was published in 2016. She has won several awards for her journalism, including the 2013 International Women of Courage Award.

LILA AZAM ZANGANEH is a writer raised in Paris, France, by exiled Iranian parents. She is the author of *The Enchanter: Nabokov and Happiness* (Norton), and recipient of the 2011 Roger Shattuck Prize for Criticism. She lives and works in New York City.

JEFFREY ZUCKERMAN's translations from French include Ananda Devi's *Eve Out of Her Ruins* (Deep Vellum, 2016) and Antoine Volodine's *Radiant Terminus* (Open Letter, 2017), as well as numerous texts by Marie Darrieussecq, Hervé Guibert, Régis Jauffret, Kaija Saariaho, and others. A graduate of Yale University, he has published writing and translations in *Best European Fiction*, *Los Angeles Review of Books*, *The Paris Review Daily*, *Tin House*, and *Vice*.

ACKNOWLEDGMENTS

"The Great Wall" and "The Wall" are excerpted from *The Ghosts of Birds* (2016), and appear courtesy of New Directions Books.

"Samiya Schmidt" is excerpted from *Radiant Terminus* (2017), and appears courtesy of Open Letter Books.

"Maureen" is excerpted from *Cities I've Never Lived In*. Originally published in *Longreads*. Copyright © 2016 by Sara Majka. Reprinted with the permission of The Permissions Company, Inc., on behalf of Graywolf Press.

"Lukin's Bed" appears courtesy of Dalkey Archive Press, which previously published this story in *Best of Contemporary Mexican Fiction* (2009).

"Marooned" is excerpted from *Wide Sargasso Sea* (1966), and appears courtesy of W. W. Norton.

"The Imagining of It" is excerpted from *See Now Then* (2013), and appears courtesy of FSG.

"Last Night, I Was Trapped in the Wrong Body Again" appears courtesy of Bull City Press, which previously published this poem in the chapbook *What Are We Not For* (2016).

"Pronunciation: Part One" appears courtesy of YesYes Books, which previously published this poem in the collection *i be, but i ain't* (2016).

"From *Charcoal Joe*" is excerpted from *Charcoal Joe: An Easy Rawlins Mystery* (2016), and appears courtesy of Penguin Random House.

Gabriel Orozco's art appears courtesy of the Marian Goodman Gallery.

Salman Rushdie's excerpt of *The Ground Beneath Her Feet* appears courtesy of the author.

"A Live Dog Being Better Than a Dead Lion" appears courtesy of BOA Editions, Ltd., which previously published this poem in the collection *Song* (1995).

"The Shootings" is excerpted from *A Meal in Winter* (2012), and appears courtesy of The New Press.

"Master Film" is excerpted from *Look* (2016), and appears courtesy of Graywolf Press.

THE GEORGIA REVIEW

LORAINE WILLIAMS POETRY PRIZE

an annual award of $1000 and publication in the Spring issue of *The Georgia Review* for a single poem. The submission period for the 2017 award opens 1 April and closes 15 May. See our site for details.

Judged by Naomi Shihab Nye

Congratulations to
Emily Wolahan

Winner of the 2016
Loraine Williams Poetry Prize

WSQ

A vital resource for research, education, and activism, *WSQ* combines contemporary developments in feminist theory and scholarship with essays, reviews, poetry, fiction, creative nonfiction, and the visual arts.

QUEER METHODS
Edited by Matt Brim & Amin Ghaziani

As Queer Studies experiences a methodological renaissance, we look to the ways that the discipline's inherent resistance, impreciseness, and provocation toward established protocols might affect its development. This issue reframes the question "what is queer theory," to "*how* is the work of queer theory done?"

VOL 44, NOs 3&4: FALL/WINTER 2016 – ISBN: 978-1-55861-942-5

AT SEA
Edited by Terri Gordon-Zolov & Amy Sodaro

The high seas are a locus of migrant and refugee crossings, lawlessness, and of environmental destruction. Academics mobilize the motif of "at sea" on a literal or figurative level, submerging in its flow of ever-changing political processes. A place of transformation, in-betweens, and movement, the ocean unites and divides us, shaping us as nations and individuals.

VOL 45, NOs 1&2: SPRING/SUMMER 2017 – ISBN: 978-1-55861-420-8

1-year subscription: Individuals, $60.00 / Institutions, $85.00. Surface mail outside the US, add: $40.00. To subscribe, visit our website, or call 212-817-7918, or email sales@feministpress.org. To advertise, email marketing@feministpress.org.

FEMINISTPRESS.ORG FP

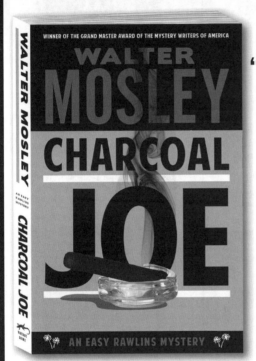

Fearless Fiction from The New Press

LONGLISTED FOR THE MAN BOOKER INTERNATIONAL PRIZE

BLACK MOSES Alain Mabanckou

A rollicking new novel from "Africa's Samuel Beckett . . . one of the continent's greatest living writers" (*The Guardian*)

"A delicious and delicate novel." —*Le Monde*

A MEAL IN WINTER Hubert Mingarelli

Shortlisted for the 2014 Independent Foreign Fiction Prize and called a "best winter read" by *The Independent*, a haunting, suspenseful novel about three German soldiers in World War II

"A reminder of the power a short, perfect work of fiction can wield." —*The Wall Street Journal*

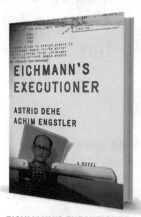

EICHMANN'S EXECUTIONER
Astrid Dehe and Achim Engstler

A gripping and beautifully imagined work of literary fiction that explores history and memory and the traumatic legacy of the Holocaust

"A fascinating book that doesn't let you go." —*Neues Deutschland*

BIRTH OF A DREAM WEAVER
Ngũgĩ wa Thiong'o

From one of the world's greatest writers, the story of how the author found his voice as a novelist at Makerere University in Uganda

"Exquisite in its honesty and truth and resilience, and a necessary chronicle from one of the greatest writers of our time." —Chimamanda Ngozi Adichie, *The Guardian*, Best Books of 2016